MAKING AFFIRMATIVE
ACTION WORK

A SOUTH AFRICAN GUIDE

RESEARCH GROUP

Mandla Adonisi – Adonisi and Associates Consultants
Najwah Allie-Edries – Development Bank of Southern Africa
Angus Bowmaker-Falconer – Graduate School of Business,
   University of Cape Town
Jeanne Gamble – Department of Adult Education and Extra-Mural Studies,
   University of Cape Town
Warren Krafchik – Institute for Democracy in South Africa (IDASA)
Peliwe Lolwana – Independent Examinations Board
Mare Norval – Mare Norval and Associates Personnel Consultants
Shelley van der Merwe – Independent researcher
Caroline White – Centre for Policy Studies

ACKNOWLEDGEMENTS

This book was made possible by generous donations from the Ford Foundation
and the Royal Danish Embassy in conjunction with the Danish International
Development Agency (Danida).

MAKING AFFIRMATIVE ACTION WORK

ACTION WORK

A SOUTH AFRICAN GUIDE

PUBLISHED BY IDASA

MAY 1995

Published by the Institute for Democracy in South Africa,
Albion Spring, 183 Main Road, Rondebosch, Cape Town 7700.

© IDASA 1995

ISBN 1-874864-14-4

First published 1995.

Cover and text design by Manik Design, Cape Town.

Typeset in Bodoni Book.

Print and bound by Creda Press, Epping, Cape Town.

TABLE OF CONTENTS

PREFACE

The mission of the Institute for Democracy in South Africa (Idasa) is to foster and strengthen a culture of democracy. Strategically, this requires the organisation to identify the critical stumbling blocks to democracy and develop and initiate programmes aimed at their resolution. South Africa's recent election has ensured greater equality in the distribution of political power. International and local attention is thus justifiably refocusing on the massive imbalances that remain in the distribution of economic resources. This challenge is central to the mission of Idasa, given the positive relationship that has been shown to exist globally between economic and political democracy. It is in this context that Idasa welcomes and participates in the debate and practise of affirmative action as one of the critical mechanisms available to support democratic transformation in South Africa. Idasa offices around the country have received an increasing of telephone calls from people who want advice about implementing affirmative action in their organisations. So great has been the demand that funds were raised to produce this "how to" book.

Eight organisations allowed a case study to be researched and written up on the history and present status of affirmative action in the work-place. The relationship with these organisations and their employees was an interactive one in which the results of the case study were fed back to interviewees and other interested parties.

South Africa does not have a rich history of transparency and accountability. Academic and industry journals seldom present current, critical case studies from which other organisations may learn. It is with gratitude, therefore, that we publish these case studies. The organisations that have participated have taken a brave stance on transparency and we hope that their example will encourage other public and private organisations to consider sharing their experiences.

The research team consisted of nine people – all involved in the field of affirmative action – including personnel practitioners and researchers. They were brought together at a workshop in Cape Town to exchange initial ideas and consensus was reached on how to conceptualise affirmative action, and on the shape and content of the book. Of the nine who attended the first and subsequent workshops and who researched and wrote the case studies, four took responsibility for the final content. They introduced the case studies, drew out their lessons and compiled the practical handbook. The book thus reflects the collaborative views of a group of people and not those of any individual or of Idasa.

Warren Krafchik
May, 1995

PART ONE

AFFIRMATIVE ACTION IN SOUTH ARICA

CHAPTER 1

HOW DO WE THINK ABOUT AFFIRMATIVE ACTION?

Very few people in South Africa today are neutral about affirmative action. Both advocates and detractors hold strong, even emotional, views and these are fuelled by myths about affirmative action. As a result, debates on the subject are muddied by the unspoken beliefs of those who hold different points of view.

On the one hand, there are those who think, for example, that supporters of affirmative action would rather appoint unqualified black people or women than qualified white men. On the other hand, ardent supporters of affirmative action often attack any queries about it as racist and/or sexist.

Those who are opposed to affirmative action condemn it as window-dressing, the fulfilment of quotas, a numbers game. They say it results in the promotion of incompetents and blocks the promising careers of young whites. They label it reverse discrimination and tokenism and say it is embarrassing and demeaning for blacks and women who are labelled "affirmative action appointments". Above all, it is dismissed as bad for business: appointing staff according to criteria other than merit reduces productivity and will hamper South Africa's economic recovery and ability to compete in the world economy.

Before we get into the main body of this work-book, it is necessary to dispel some of these myths that hamper the implementation of affirmative action. In particular, we will look at whether affirmative action is responsible for the evils attributed to it like lowering standards and abolishing merit as a criterion for appointment and promotion. We will also look at some other contentious issues: whether there is such a person as an "affirmative action candidate"; whether individuals or organisations are the targets; whether affirmative action should target only Africans, all black people, or women as well; and whether there is any end point to affirmative action.

The affirmative action now being implemented in South Africa is not in response to legislation, though that could come later. No quotas are yet being imposed on employers, some of whom are setting their own targets in order to drive, and then measure, their performance.

This is not the first time that affirmative action has been implemented in this country. For many years, white Afrikaners (mainly men) were pushed ahead via the Broederbond, the civil service and the parastatal employers. Many of the myths that we are hearing now were created when affirmative action for poor white Afrikaners was mooted in the early years of this century. A 1904 Transvaal Mines Commission report said that Afrikaners were "incompetent and apathetic indigents" who "can hardly be considered in efficiency the equal of a native"[1]. Yet these same pariahs were turned into skilled and efficient mine workers and managers. The case studies in this book suggest that similar outcomes are possible now, contradicting affirmative action's sceptics.

The debate about affirmative action has, unfortunately, collapsed into a binary opposition: the detractors see nothing good and the supporters nothing

---

1. *Cited by the late housing minister, Joe Slovo,* Business Day, *4 September 1992.*

bad. If we are going to implement affirmative action successfully, we need to examine our own attitudes. We start here by raising a few questions that the reader will explore when reading the book. We are not going to begin with a definition because definitions are easy to fault and discard. Since employers are feeling some pressure to embark on affirmative action, we will start with the question: Is affirmative action necessary?

IS AFFIRMATIVE ACTION NECESSARY?

THE LEGISLATIVE FRAMEWORK

According to the new constitution, unfair discrimination in the work-place on irrelevant grounds (race, sex, disability, etc.) is illegal. A person who believes he/she has been unfairly discriminated against is entitled to seek relief through an Equality Commission, the Constitutional Court or the ordinary courts. Where there has been overt, provable discrimination there is likely to be a finding in his/her favour.

In addition, there will probably be a remedy for what is called "systemic discrimination". Here a person will argue in court that there has been discrimination on the basis of membership of a group which statistics demonstrate to be under-represented in their organisation.

For example, the only qualification for being a delivery driver is the possession of a clean and valid driving licence. Yet, if we look at the distribution of drivers in any company in South Africa, they are almost certain to be all men. No particular woman who applied for the job has been turned down, probably because none have applied knowing that women are never employed as drivers. This is why one needs affirmative action with special advertising, for example, to get them to apply. But, using the figures, one would be able to argue conclusively in court that there has been "systemic discrimination" against women being employed as drivers.

The prevalence of systemic discrimination is due to the fact that, despite a personal commitment by some managers to non-racialism and non-sexism, managers continue to be prejudiced against women and blacks in ways that they do not recognise as prejudice. This results in persistent differentiation in the labour market that disadvantages women and blacks. In a study of 306 business people, 98 percent of whom were white and 95 percent male, P Human and K Hofmeyr found:

> Whilst the majority felt that business and society should accept blacks (women),
> value their work and provide equal opportunities for them, the majority also felt
> that blacks (women) do not have the objectivity to evaluate business situations
> properly and just less than half felt that blacks (women) are too emotional and
> that challenging work is not that important to blacks (women) as it is to whites
> (men). The respondents also had problems with the self-confidence of blacks

(women) as well as their ability to contribute as much as whites (men) to the overall goals of the organisation. Although three-quarters felt that blacks (women) have the capability to acquire the skills necessary for management positions, only half felt that blacks (women) are as capable as whites (men) of learning mathematical and mechanical skills[2].

Both of these kinds of discrimination (direct and systemic) are relatively easy to demonstrate. What is more difficult is showing, for example, that women or black people are being discriminated against because they are not being paid equally for work of equal value. Women and men, blacks and whites, are usually employed to carry out very different tasks that are difficult to compare. However, such discrimination is bound to be covered by equality legislation and companies with segregated work-forces may soon find themselves under threat of prosecution.

This is one reason why companies might put affirmative action processes in place. They want to deflect the heavy legal and compensation costs of being found guilty of discrimination by trying to ensure that black people and women are represented at all levels and in all disciplines roughly according to the demography of the country.

FINANCIAL INCENTIVES FOR AFFIRMATIVE ACTION

Affirmative action has also become essential because of changes in the demand for goods and services. A company that wants to take advantage of the increased buying power of blacks must adapt its organisation to ensure success. Alternatively, companies will feel consumer pressure to make their work-force match more closely the composition of their customer base. This is clearly the case in South Africa where most of the firms in the case studies can trace their affirmative action initiatives to a rapid change in their consumer base.

A further hard-headed business reason for implementing affirmative action is that the country cannot afford to go on wasting the talents and potential of the black and female components of our population. There is a shortage of technical and managerial skills in our economy that can no longer be compensated for in the old way – by importing skilled, white men. It is politically impossible, morally indefensible and economically short-sighted. South Africa ranks 14th (last) on human resources development in the *World Competitiveness Report* (1994). There are also serious and growing shortages of necessary skills. In addition, affirmative action is part of the Reconstruction and Development Programme, a nation-wide initiative to which all the major business groupings have pledged their support.

---

2. *Human, P and K Hofmeyr. 1987 "Attitudes of South African managers to the advancement of blacks in business" in* South African Journal of Labour Relations, *Vol 11, No 3: 5-19. The substitution of women and men for blacks and whites will prove our point that racism and sexism produce similar prejudices against the "other" group.*

AN ISSUE OF JUSTICE

Another reason for implementing affirmative action is often dismissed as idealistic, namely justice. Colonialism, sexism and apartheid in South Africa prevented black people and women of all races from getting an equal education and an equal opportunity to compete in the labour market. There is an argument that affirmative action is necessary because simply taking away the obvious barriers to the appointment and promotion of black people and women will make little difference to the effects of past discrimination and of systemic discrimination in an organisation. This is a situation that we can no longer afford, morally, politically or economically.

MYTHS AND MISCONCEPTIONS

THE MYTH OF MERIT

When affirmative action is discussed, someone is sure to ask: Doesn't affirmative action mean that standards will fall because race or gender are being substituted for merit (qualifications plus experience) as the criterion for appointment or promotion?

If the results of the Human and Hofmeyr study still hold true (as they probably do), one can question whether the much vaunted "merit principle" is being applied when blacks (or women) are evaluated for appointment or promotion by the majority of white (male) managers. The idea of "merit" – that the person with the highest qualifications and the most experience for the job must be appointed – is superficially unassailable. However, there are some serious issues to be raised about the neutrality of the concept "merit". A person's relative merit in relation to a vacancy or promotion is commonly understood to be based on their ability or capacity (including potential) to perform in that position. But the quotation from Human and Hofmeyr above suggests that merit is not currently the sole, or even the critical, criterion for selection and promotion. On the contrary, perceptions of the stereotypes associated with (white) men on the one hand and women and blacks on the other strongly influence the assessment of merit. These stereotypes include what women and blacks are thought to be capable of and what kinds of work are considered suitable for them.

As a result, people who make selections for positions and promotions make decisions that are not necessarily consistent with the merit principle. In reality, people prefer to give jobs to people like themselves. As a result, there is a bias in favour of people similar to the selectors, most commonly white males. This is not easily detected as outright discrimination, but nonetheless results in appointments which do not conform to the merit principle.

In some cases there is also a tendency among employers, especially where the job entails contact with the public, to employ people who conform to consumer expectations. This may lead to the exclusive appointment of conventionally attractive young women as receptionists, airline cabin staff, etc or of white men in positions of authority because customers refuse to deal with women. Again, the merit principle is over-ridden by other considerations that have nothing to do with ability to perform the task.

It can be argued, therefore, that affirmative action policies that contain measures to over-ride these conventional criteria for appointment actually enshrine rather than displace the merit principle. They ensure that only relevant and appropriate criteria are used for appointments and promotions, and that proper consideration is given to all qualified candidates, regardless of gender and race.

To achieve this, the merit principle needs to be redefined as:

> Revision of standards and practices and selection criteria to ensure that they do not exclude qualified people from consideration for positions and employment benefits. This involves not only removing arbitrary, artificial and unnecessary barriers to employment opportunities, but a reassessment of current standards so that a more realistic interpretation of what "merit" actually involves for particular jobs or benefits is applied[3].

Affirmative action can, it is argued, ensure that there will in fact be equal employment opportunities. In addition, positive discrimination in favour of white men – in other words, appointing "somebody like us", "somebody who will fit in", "somebody with whom we will feel comfortable" – will then in time cease. The unfortunate alternative to this is that the system will continue to reproduce the present inequalities by violating the merit principle. The consequence of a move away from importing skills and promoting "somebody like us" is that, at a certain point, there will be enough black people and women to ensure that the organisational culture is no longer predominantly white and male.

Can an organisation survive this transformation and remain efficient?This type of consideration is a key concern for many companies and organisations. For example, it has been asked: What about "African time"? What about women's other responsibilities? What about the loss of skills and expertise that has been accumulated by the senior members of staff?

In the long term, affirmative action is probably a requirement for efficiency in South Africa. Our history has shown that inefficiency is not an inevitable consequence of affirmative action – the example of affirmative action for Afrikaners, mentioned above, is a case in point. The critical issue is not whether to have affirmative action but how to introduce it, and that is the subject of this book. Based on nine case studies of South African companies and organisations that have already embarked on implementing affirmative action policies, this book shows there are no easy answers to these questions.

---

3. Burton, C. 1988. *"Redefining merit." Canberra: Affirmative Action Agency, Monograph No 2.*

WHO ARE THE BENEFICIARIES?

INDIVIDUALS OR ORGANISATIONS?

How often have you heard the following:

> Of course, Themba was an affirmative action appointment.

> How many affirmative action candidates have you got on the shortlist?

> I don't want the promotion if I'm going to be called an affirmative action appointment.

> That job is earmarked as an affirmative action position.

These kinds of comments have become commonplace in South Africa over the last few years. People who are called affirmative action appointees reject the label and assert that they got the job on merit. Nonetheless, it is easy to slip into this terminology and most people do not question this approach.

In contrast to this unreflective use of a careless shorthand is a view that once an organisation has an affirmative action policy in place it becomes an affirmative action organisation where each and every promotion or appointment is conducted in terms of the policy. Every staff movement, even of a white male, is then subject to the affirmative action policy. The white male is then also an affirmative action promotion, even if it is a move sideways to gain more experience or to make room for a woman or a black man who can do his job. Once this language is adopted and the notion of an affirmative action organisation is accepted, no one will have to defend themselves against inaccurate and demeaning labels. Everyone will have been appointed or promoted on merit, not on the basis of "who you know" but rather on carefully constructed criteria for the position which will have been developed as part of the affirmative action programme.

Affirmative action can therefore be seen simply as a process confined to employment and promotion practices, or it can be viewed as the overall transformation of an organisation in an increasingly desirable direction.

AFRICANS OR BLACKS?

Readers will have noticed that the word "blacks" is used here without reference to the old apartheid categories of "blacks, coloureds and Asians". However, this is not an uncontested term. Many supporters of affirmative action for those disadvantaged by apartheid feel that there were degrees of disadvantage which ought to be recognised. The apartheid hierarchy had whites at the top, then Asians, coloureds and, finally, Africans. The differences were emphasised in material ways. Less funding was provided for education down the scale. There were smaller pensions, less housing provision and, of course, job reservation and the coloured labour preference policies.

For many, Africans are not only the most disadvantaged but also the overwhelming majority whose needs ought to be catered for first. Once they are on the way to equality, the argument goes, we can think about other, less disadvantaged groups.

There is some interesting statistical support for this position: white men make up about 9 percent of the population, yet they provide 75 percent of managers. They are thus over-represented by about 67 percent. This explains why affirmative action programmes are often implemented at this level. Asian men are also over-represented – by about 4 percent – but on a very small base of only 1.5 percent of the population[4]. These are national figures and could, of course, look even more striking if one were to isolate the figures for Asian men in Natal or coloured men in the Western Cape.

These are some of the issues that organisations will have to consider in the process of initiating affirmative action programmes and consulting with their stakeholders on these.

AND WOMEN?

Those who support the "Africanist" position outlined above often have little sympathy for the disadvantage suffered by women. Many take the view (which is incorrect) that most women are not breadwinners and therefore do not need the same support as (black) men to obtain equal job opportunities. They often share the prejudices against women's competence expressed in the quotation from Human and Hofmeyr above.

There is another argument which says that white women do not need affirmative action because they are already sufficiently represented in the work-force. The statistics support this view: at management level white women are over-represented to the same degree as Asian men. However, they are seriously under-represented at senior manager and director levels, as are Asian women.

The most under-represented group at this level is, of course, African women. Consequently, it is argued, if there is to be any affirmative action directed at women it should target African women only. Those who care about equality for women fear that black men will substitute for white men in the new dispensation. African women will not make it into the better paid levels of organisations, and will continue to earn less than men for work of equal value. There is also concern about the fact that there are almost no women (black or white) mechanical and electronic engineers and no women artisans or apprentices in South Africa at all.

---

4. *Crankshaw, O and D Hindson, cited in C White. 1993.* Status of South African Women: A Source Book in Tables and Graphs. *Johannesburg: ANC Women's League.*

DO 'FOREIGN BLACKS' COUNT?

Even more divisive is the question of whether citizens of other African countries or blacks from the United States or elsewhere should also be targets of affirmative action, or only those who were affected by apartheid and destabilisation.

Some feel that citizens from neighbouring countries should be counted as victims of apartheid and allowed to enjoy our relative economic prosperity. Others, however, passionately believe that we cannot accommodate foreigners, no matter how disadvantaged or how qualified, while 50 percent of our own citizens are unemployed.

WHAT IS THE END POINT OF AFFIRMATIVE ACTION?

IS IT ABOUT NUMBERS?

The Black Management Forum (BMF) and others have stated categorically that the goal of affirmative action is the fair representation of all sectors of South African society at all levels and in all fields in proportion to their presence in the population.

However, the BMF believes that affirmative action programmes will no longer be necessary and should be ended once a "critical mass" of the decision-makers in an organisation come from previously under-represented categories. Selection processes can then take place "naturally" without policy intervention.

OR ABOUT TRANSFORMATION?

Is the organisation going to adapt to its new decision-makers or will they be expected to conform to the existing ethos? On the one hand, people who are already there are likely to want to stay within their "comfort zone" – there should not be too much change so they no longer recognise their place of work. On the other hand, women and black men often feel uncomfortable with the white male culture that dominates in most organisations and companies. They are excluded from the conventional sporting and drinking activities where important discussions often take place and they will never be "one of the boys".

Besides, many of them argue, what is so good about the uptight, stiff-upper-lip, efficiency-at-all-costs atmosphere that this culture implies? An injection of "*ubuntu*" and "womanly values" might make our organisations more co-operative, participatory and productive.

When the organisational culture (however measured) has been transformed, affirmative action has done its job.

ONLY AT THE TOP?

Some organisations may view affirmative action as a mechanism for
transforming management and for bringing people from under-represented
categories on to the boards and governing bodies of organisations. Some
companies deliberately limit their actions to this sector. This involves selecting
people who already have the skills or the potential to be appointed or promoted
into managerial and higher technical positions. Bursaries for university
courses in technical skills and management are often part of these
organisations' strategy, combined with internal training and career pathing. On
the other hand, unions and other organisations argue that affirmative action
should not be a process that creates an elite through upward mobility only for
the few. Unions that have taken up this issue – the National Union of
Metalworkers of SA (Numsa) in particular – argue that affirmative action
should be a policy, arrived at by negotiation, that is applicable to all members
of a work-force. It should include and differentiate between those who need
literacy training to start off their careers and those who could benefit from
more advanced courses.

In addition, if existing employees are not considered for advancement, the
organisation is not developing mechanisms to reproduce itself and to ensure
that it has the right people for top jobs in the future.

The issue is by no means simple. Recruitment to top positions in some
organisations has traditionally targeted only university or technikon graduates.
In others, this practice is relatively recent and a response to several factors,
including affirmative action, which makes it no longer possible to rely on
networks. Whatever the origin, the consequence is that it is almost unheard of
in South Africa for a person to rise from the shop floor to top management.
Even though it might have been possible in the past for a white artisan to
follow this route, there have been virtually no black artisans until very
recently. It is therefore argued that affirmative action should not be confined to
management. At the same time, there should also be affirmative action to
ensure that women and blacks get fair access to apprenticeships. They should
also be given a continuous career path through supervision or junior
management into the top management. Another measure of the success of
affirmative action would therefore be how many people at the top of an
organisation started their career at the bottom.

Affirmative action can be seen as part of an overall transformation or as a
process confined to employment and promotion practices. Similarly,
affirmative action can be seen as one of a number of personnel policies. Or it
can be viewed as only one part of a considered transformation process aimed at
developing all employees to the point where each is able to make their greatest
contribution to the overall performance of the organisation. The question that
an organisation has to ask itself is whether affirmative action is a matter of
appointments and promotions, or a question of overall transformation.

WHAT IS AFFIRMATIVE ACTION: A DEFINITION

In the light of the above, we can now propose a working definition that will be useful in reading this book and in formulating a statement of intent:

> Affirmative action is a process designed to achieve equal employment opportunities. In order to achieve this goal, the barriers in the work-place which restrict employment and progression opportunities have to be systematically eliminated[5].

THE STRUCTURE OF THE BOOK

Because this book has been written in response to requests for help, it has been designed to provide what we hope is sufficient useful information to answer readers' queries and meet their objectives.

The substance of the book starts in Chapter Two with the case studies. This is essential reading because it gives us the history of all the activities that have fallen under the label "affirmative action", including what long ago might have been called "black advancement" or some other such term. What interested us, and what we hope you will find useful is how, in some cases, problems were detected in these early efforts and how they were evaluated and changed. In other cases, affirmative action seemed a fairly ad hoc process, depending on individual enthusiasm, responsibilities and staff changes. The emphasis in the case studies is on process, and not on the perfect model. Nobody has a perfect programme, but everybody who has participated in this book has felt that their approach, whether it be intuitive or systematic, has something to teach those who have just embarked on the journey.

In Part Two, we guide you through the process of setting up an affirmative action policy for your organisation. Chapter Three is a conceptual chapter in which we synthesise the observations from the case studies into a set of principles that we suggest underpin affirmative action. Chapter Four offers a step-by-step user guide, compatible with the principles above, to draft an affirmative action policy uniquely suited to your own organisation. ■

---

5.   *Adapted from the Australian Affirmative Action (Equal Opportunity for Women) Act, 1986.*

■ CHAPTER 2 ■

THE CASE STUDIES

SOUTH AFRICAN BREWERIES
BEER DIVISION

CAROLINE WHITE

PROFILE OF THE COMPANY

> We are changing so much, so fast, in this company that a senior chap who went
> on a course for a year needed six months re-orientation when he came back! (An
> SAB general manager.)

This comment was not just about the rapid changes being wrought under the
aegis of the affirmative action or "Equity" programme. It was also an
observation that the top and middle managers of South African Breweries
(SAB) are, at any single moment, driving several initiatives simultaneously,
each interacting with, and, more rarely, competing with the others. The
company also has a 20-year history of implementing affirmative action in
various forms.

SAB Beer Division has a top management team of extraordinary self-
confidence, energy and enthusiasm. The management also prides itself on the
intelligence of its members and their dynamic commitment to change and
progress. An overwhelming impression created by all the salaried staff who
were interviewed, black and white, men and women, was that what they most
appreciated about their jobs was the "constant challenge". How was this
buoyant and optimistic frame of mind, coupled with innovation, possible in the
then depressed state of the South African economy?

One reason is that SAB enjoys a 90 percent share of the clear beer market
and it is almost impossible for new entrants to make a dent in the giant's sales
figures. Louis Luyt tried it and failed in the 1970s. National Sorghum
Breweries recently launched Vivo clear beer after several delays. It is too soon
to assess its impact on the SAB market, but the ability of Bavaria Brau to
compete with major sellers like Castle and Lion appears limited, to say the
least.

Lower-level employees agreed that change was a constant at SAB and that something new was always being introduced on the shop floor. For example, in early 1994 when these interviews took place, SAB had recently introduced its own innovative management programme, World Class Manufacturing and Performance Management, at all plants. At Alrode, in Alberton, a new packaging line was being developed which would fill as many bottles as the whole plant at Newlands, Cape Town: 60 000 bottles per hour. With this proliferation of new ideas and objectives, affirmative action could easily have been sidelined in favour of management's more traditional concerns – costs and productivity. In fact it is today one of the five business imperatives of the company.

However, as in most organisations, not everybody shares the same positive approach. For example, a senior black manager said:

> When you sit in management meetings there are certain things that are said and certain things which are not said in your (ie a black person's) presence. And you know very well that it will be discussed either in the pub or on Sundays when the guys get together and you are not part of that scene.

Many interviewees, both women and men, also said the company was very "macho". This was attributed to the fact that "the company's product is sold mainly to men", even though a high proportion of consumers are female. Its staff was therefore overwhelmingly male.

Finally, SAB is characterised by a high level of commitment to affirmative action, which it calls "Equity". It has had considerable success in achieving the targets that it set itself in 1985 and again in 1991. In 1971, only 1 percent of SAB's salaried employees were black. By 1978, this proportion had risen to 13 percent and by 1985 to 28 percent. By 1993, 48 percent of the salaried staff at SAB Beer Division were what SAB insiders refer to as "ABCs" (Asians, Blacks and Coloureds), referred to in this study as blacks.

Further evidence of commitment to the project was the company's expenditure on training, which "equals Japanese levels as a percentage of turnover", according to an SAB manager. However, the black employees were not evenly spread through all levels of salaried staff as the table overleaf demonstrates.

METHOD AND SAMPLE

The researcher contacted the manager responsible for affirmative action at the SAB Beer Division head office in December 1993 and arranged to carry out the research early in 1994. SAB Beer Division is an enormous company with a huge staff complement located at many breweries and distribution centres throughout the country. It is divided into several regions, each of which has its own ethos. Logistically, it was possible to focus on only two regions and on only

■ TABLE 1 ■

PERMANENT STAFF STRENGTH BY RACE, GENDER AND SKILL LEVEL. MARCH 31, 1994.

PATERSON GRADE	WHITE	AFRICAN	COLOURED	ASIAN	TOTAL	WOMEN
NON-EXEC DIR						
F		1			1	
E 4-5	6				6	
E 1-3	65	3			68	1
D 4-5	177	15	1	3	196	6
D 1-3	459	91	17	32	599	81
C 4-5	204	84	14	23	325	74
C 1-3	542	454	89	101	1 186	235
B	585	2 914	294	136	3 929	503
A	26	2 850	109	31	3 016	33
UNGRADED	1	4			5	
TOTAL	2 066	6 415	524	326	9 331	933

Source: UCT Graduate School of Business — Breakwater Monitor

Notes:

Paterson F	Executive Directors
Paterson E 4-5	Senior — Executive Management
Paterson E 1-3	Senior Management
Paterson D 4-5	Middle — Senior Management
Paterson D 1-3	Junior — Middle Management
Paterson C 4-5	Assistant Management — Senior Supervisory & Junior Professional
Paterson C 1-3	Graduate Entry, Supervisory, Artisan & Technician, Senior Operative & Senior Admin/Clerical/Secretarial
Paterson B	Operative, Admin/Clerical/Secretarial
Paterson A	Entry Level Operative & Labourer

one site within each.

Interviews were conducted during January and February at the head office in Sandton, near Johannesburg and at the production plants in Cape Town and Alrode. In addition, the general manager at United Breweries, GaRankuwa, was interviewed as the highest placed black manager in the company. He is now regional general manager for the Northern Transvaal and, as an executive member of the board of directors since July 1994, is the highest ranking black person in the company. I also interviewed the retired human resources director who had been responsible for the first moves into affirmative action at the SAB Beer Division and who had continued to be involved in the programme.

I indicated the spread of people I would like to interview and the interviewees were selected by the human resource managers at Cape Town and Alrode and by the affirmative action manager at head office. At the production sites, I was provided with an office to conduct the pre-arranged schedule of interviews. I was also given a guided tour of both breweries.

The following table shows the spread of staff with whom interviews were conducted. The black shop floor staff interviewed in both Cape Town and Alrode were shop stewards from the Food and Allied Workers' Union (Fawu), a Congress of South African Trade Union affiliate.

■ TABLE 2 ■

		MANAGERS	SUPERVISORS & ARTISANS	SHOP FLOOR	TOTAL
CENTRAL OFFICE:	BLACK WOMEN				
	BLACK MEN	2			2
	WHITE WOMEN	2			2
	WHITE MEN	2			2
ALRODE:	BLACK WOMEN				
	BLACK MEN	4	3	2	9
	WHITE WOMEN	1			1
	WHITE MEN	5	2		7
CAPE TOWN:	BLACK WOMEN		1		1
	BLACK MEN	4		4	8
	WHITE WOMEN	1			1
	WHITE MEN	5	1		6
TOTAL		26	7	6	39

HISTORY OF EQUITY/AFFIRMATIVE ACTION AT SAB

A quite remarkable figure of 48 percent of salaried staff at SAB are black, and the number is still increasing. SAB has a long record of concern about the employment of blacks at levels above the shop floor and there has been a high level of commitment to affirmative action by successive managing directors.

The library at SAB group headquarters has a record of every speech and policy document on affirmative action. Using these, Joe Horner, former personnel director, produced a summary of the development of the Beer Division's commitment to equal opportunity. He divided this development into three phases:

PHASE 1:
AFRICANISATION AND BLACK ADVANCEMENT (1971 – 1985)

In 1971, Horner presented his annual report to the board and argued that something needed to be done to promote "the optimum use of African labour". Influenced by this report, SAB produced a plan for the Africanisation of the company in 1972. To start the process, systematic reports on human resources were compiled each year until 1975 and in 1976 targets for Africanisation over the next three years were set for the first time. During the period from 1971 to 1985, the number of blacks in salaried employment at the Beer Division increased from 37 to 840, or from 1 percent to 28 percent. They were predominantly in the lower grades with very few senior appointments. For example, by 1983 there were 18 senior managers (Paterson D1-3) or 6 percent of the total who were blacks, and 15 or 9 percent of middle managers (Patterson D4-5). There were no blacks at executive level (Paterson E+).

It is clear that top management realised that having a policy for Africanisation or black advancement was not enough to produce the results needed, especially in view of the "facts of the market": that 80 percent of their consumers were, and still are, black.

Research was undertaken to establish the best way to increase the number of blacks in salaried posts. This included visits to other breweries in southern Africa and looking at what a range of other organisations were doing. The summary report of this research lists various "do's and don't's", many of which became cornerstones of the Beer Division's later policy.

These included: set targets, numbers, jobs etc; make it a line management project included in line managers' objectives, with rewards and punishments; identify target jobs and train blacks to fill them; put blacks into line jobs with authority and responsibility; have career plans for whites as well as blacks; prioritise getting the company climate right to support the programme. It is remarkable how closely this list of recommendations resembles some of the most advanced thinking in the field today.

Some of its critics have argued that SAB had it easy in the affirmative action game. It was so profitable that it simply increased the pay roll figures and made new jobs for blacks. While it is true that SAB has been profitable since 1971, there was no evidence that this influenced the decision to evaluate and upgrade the Africanisation policy. In order to keep up with demand for its product, SAB expanded its capacity and this created some new posts. The increase in the number of jobs was driven by the need for real new positions and not by any desire to create token posts to be filled by blacks who did nothing but enhance the company image.

On the contrary, the main influence on the drive for affirmative action in the next period was Peter Lloyd, then the newly appointed chief executive. He was not prepared to create phoney jobs for blacks. In his view, everyone had to have a real job in which she or he was evaluated by common standards of performance. In this and other matters concerning affirmative action, he was positively influenced by Horner's work in the previous phase and, in particular, the results of a serious evaluation of what had gone before.

PHASE 2:
THE EQUITY POLICY, LATER KNOWN AS EQUITY I (1985 – 1992)

The most significant development of this phase was that affirmative action was placed on a par with the other main business strategies of the Beer Division: marketing, quality, unit costs and people. The managing director put his authority and commitment behind it and allocated resources so that it could be implemented. He made as many as 30 personal presentations on the policy around the country to all levels down to junior management.
In these talks he made it clear that managers' advancement and bonuses would depend as much on performance in this area as on performance in sales and costs. The responsibility for the success of the programme was placed on the shoulders of line management, with human resources personnel playing a supporting role through advice, training, selection procedures and, above all, testing.
    A long-standing SAB tradition of systematic testing of candidates for appointment and advancement has been incorporated into the Equity programmes. Testing is applied to whites as well as to blacks. This unique feature of SAB is perhaps related to the employment of a leading authority on psychometric testing, Dr Simon Biesheuwel, who left the Council for Scientific and Industrial Research for political reasons in the late 1950s. The person currently running the Equity programme is also a psychologist.
    The target which was set was:

> To achieve a 50/50 mix between white and non-white salaried employees on an
> integrated basis by 1990, with all employees being competent in their then
> current position. (MD's Presentation to Central Office, Regional and Sub-
> Regional Executive Teams, January 1986)

In implementing this target, managers were to pursue the following interim goals:
• By April 1989, 300 posts to be filled with blacks, according to plans which were developed at plant, regional and national level.
• By 1990, the remaining 600 posts to be filled in order to reach the 50/50 target.
• "By April 1991", the MD is reported to have said, "I don't want a single ABC who is regarded as ineffective in his job."

This was intended to, and by all accounts did, mean that people were to be properly qualified and trained for their jobs. If they could not perform to the required standard, despite support and counselling, they were to be dismissed. In this, SAB's policy and practice was that the same standards of performance were to be applied to black and white employees.

During this phase, blacks increased from the 28 percent of the work-force (840 people) in 1985 to 46 percent (1 900 people) in 1992. Thus although the target of 50 percent was not achieved, enormous progress was made. Among the reasons for this success was that the company's markets were expanding, it was building more plants and, therefore, was increasing its demand for staff. There was therefore money available to fund affirmative action and the training and mentoring that this involved. It also meant that the policy was relatively easily accepted by white employees once they saw that their own jobs were not being threatened.

A crucial component of what came to be known as Equity I (after the launch of Equity II) was supposed to be the constant monitoring of progress. During 1988, each region carried out a survey of its internal climate and these included some questions on the impact of, and attitudes towards, the Equity policy. However, a complete survey of all plants and centres throughout the country was not conducted until 1990, five years after the original launch (J Horner, interview, February 1994).

Altogether 100 blacks and 100 whites were interviewed for this company-wide survey, and while the whites said it was moving too fast, the blacks felt it was moving too slowly. There could be no avoiding the fact that some appointments had been mistakes and people had been employed who were not "effective in their posts". It also became clear that the target had not been met. Several "ineffective" black managers were dismissed in this period, as were several whites.

The 1990 survey also found that the programme had lost its impetus. There were always other demands for managers' attention and considerable difficulty in maintaining enthusiasm for a programme that, it was feared, would still have a negative impact on any manager's "bottom line": costs and productivity.

Where they could get away with it, especially where the reporting manager did not press the issue, managers were sliding out of meeting their Equity targets. They "put it on the back burner" or let it "drift to the side of the desk".

The results of these evaluations are contained in the *Equity Programme Manual 1991 - 1996* (dated April 1991). The criticisms of Equity I that were raised in this document included:

- Target-setting was too "loose", allowing for variations in interpretation of what 50 percent actually meant.
- The spread of blacks across disciplines and in the higher grades was not satisfactory: of the executives, three were in human resources, three in sales/distribution and only two in production.
- The turnover of black managers was too high.
- Many black supervisors were members of the union and following the 1989

wage strike, a "substantial number of these supervisors (black managers!) were dismissed" (emphasis in the original).

- Most of the "ABC" appointments had been external recruits rather than internal promotions.
- Many blacks had left because they felt that SAB had not fulfilled its part of the bargain.
- The programme, despite being a "full-blown organisation design/development intervention ... was not introduced or monitored as systematically as is normally the case with major organisational development programmes".
- Despite the bonus for achieving Equity targets, managers and executives were "discounting" (for example) 15 percent from their total possible earnings because they despaired of achieving the targets.

PHASE 3:
EQUITY II (1992 – THE PRESENT)

Under a new chairman, Graham Mackay (recently appointed as Group Operating Executive, SAB Group), the Equity programme was given a new impetus. His view was that the "top guy" had to make it happen because by saying simply that "it is part of our policy" nothing would get done. According to Mackay:

> You have to say to a manager 'I don't care what it takes, but in that particular position you have to have a black man' in the same way as you say 'I want X million gallons of beer brewed'. You have to have it rank with those objectives because it is so much easier to employ whites. They are easier to find, easier to acclimatise, easier to get objectives out of them because you understand how their minds work. (Interview, 12 January 1994.)

In addition to sticking to the principle of a target of 50 percent, it was recognised that what black managers there were tended to be clustered in junior and middle management. There were very few black senior managers and no executives or executive directors at board level. They were also not spread across disciplines. Most black salaried staff were in the "soft" areas of industrial relations and human resources rather than in the "hard" areas of sales, finance, engineering and general management.

Perhaps the most impressive part of Equity II was the fact that every person with line responsibility had to help draw up a staffing plan in which posts were earmarked for Equity appointments. Eligible black internal candidates also had to be targeted and provided with the necessary training, without being promised the job. Where necessary, white incumbents were moved sideways (as a form of career development by increasing their experience) to make room for a black candidate who was qualified for that particular job. According to the Equity audit carried out by the head office human resources department in late 1993, there were detailed three-year Equity plans in all plants countrywide.

A crucial new component of Equity II was "Commercial Equity". This involved assistance to selected black employees who volunteered to lease or buy their own beer delivery trucks. It was also stipulated that at least 67 percent and then an increasing proportion of "non-core" purchases had to be bought from black suppliers. Essential supplies were also made subject to comparable sourcing requirements.

Another important development alongside Equity (I and II), was the emphasis on value sharing. In a series of workshops, SAB employees together developed 10 shared values. One of the most important of these was "human dignity". This led the company to introduce to audits of all the facilities in the company, including staff canteens, changing -rooms and pubs. It also reconsidered access to personnel departments for shift workers and workers in such categories.

For example, when the change rooms at Alrode had to be enlarged to cater for more staff, the union was invited to help design them and they now include a gym.

Value sharing workshops involve staff at all branches of SAB, though numbers vary at any particular site. For example, about 28 percent of staff of all races at the Alrode plant have attended such workshops. The chairman talks about the importance of creating "a constant wash of propaganda about change" via workshops and weekends away.

There is also a video, which all employees are expected to view, designed to facilitate changes in attitude. These are all intended to create a supportive environment for Equity.

In summary, therefore, Equity II consists of a much clearer statement of objectives, actions and evaluations than the previous Equity I. According to the *Equity Programme Manual 1991 - 1996* (April 1991), its main components are:

- To affirmatively integrate employees so that they are representative of South Africa's race groups at all levels and in all disciplines. This involves setting head count targets overall and at separate levels.
- To ensure that all work practices and facilities are equitable, and are only differentiated on occupationally relevant and fair criteria. This means enhancing worker dignity by desegregating all facilities and making all personnel practices uniform.
- To be committed to the eradication of social prejudices and attitudes in the work-place that are prejudicial to, and detrimentally affect, the human dignity of any employee. This means encouraging human dignity and eliminating racist practices and language.
- To affirmatively direct our corporate social investment towards redressing past social inequities. This involves Commercial Equity or directing contracts of non-essential services and products to black-owned businesses.

EVALUATION OF THE EQUITY POLICY

LIMITED SCOPE OF POLICY

The Equity targets were limited to salaried staff. It required line managers to assist in overall target setting to increase the number of black staff in the salaried ranks. There were sections of the policy which were important on the shop floor. These included value sharing, promoting human dignity and eliminating racism. Targets were, however, not set for promotions from the shop floor, for example, nor for increasing the number of women artisans.

The only African general manager in the company argued that targets should, in future, be differentiated by discipline and by grade. Without this, targets could be fulfilled without making any advance in the number of technically trained and experienced blacks. The absence of this differentiation has led to the position where, at his site in an ex-homeland, 70 percent of the staff were black, including management, but whites still occupied all the technical jobs. The general manager was therefore over-performing in terms of the target requirements, but there was a lack of spread of the different types of skills and knowledge in the company.

Staff were aware of the limited scope of the policy and were trying to address this. Several ideas were in the pipeline: more bursaries for technical colleges, training of artisan aides, training of blacks with potential at SAB's own training centre which specialises in brewing skills, amongst others.

There has been considerable success in targeting blacks for bursaries. In 1993, 32 of the 52 bursars were black and in 1994, 50 were black. However, the rate at which "ABC" bursars take up permanent posts after their initial contract period (one year for each year of study as a bursar) was disappointing but showed signs of improving. Of the 13 blacks who completed courses in each year, six joined the permanent staff in 1993 and 11 in 1994. The figures for apprentices showed that almost 50 percent of the current intake were African.

LACK OF COMMUNICATION WITH SHOP FLOOR AND UNIONS

None of the shop stewards to whom I spoke could give a coherent account of the policy. Several said that despite the Equity policy, there were no senior black managers in their part of the company. A few had a clear understanding of the Commercial Equity section of the policy only because they sat on a committee concerned with this issue. None of them appeared to have seen the Equity video and all complained that communication on Equity was poor. An evaluation (part of a continuing series) was carried out at the end of 1993, specifically designed to expose problems. It tended to focus on this area of concern and showed that most or many shop floor workers at the time:

- Did not know there was a programme called Equity or what it was about.

- Did not know what Commercial Equity was about.
- Had not seen the Equity video.
- Felt that blacks in senior positions did not have the authority that they should have.
- Felt that whites did not respect their black colleagues, especially weekly paid employees.
- The use of derogatory language was still rife.
- There were still problems in arranging integrated functions and sports facilities[1].

The Beer Division now recognises Fawu as the sole negotiator for shop floor workers. The first agreement was negotiated in the Eastern Cape in 1983 and other regions slowly followed suit with a variety of unions. This culminated in a national agreement with Fawu in 1987. There were some long and damaging strikes in the process. Top management recognised the importance of good industrial relations and a strong bargaining unit with competent shop stewards. Union members who were interviewed, however, claimed that the union had not been consulted on Equity. Several shop stewards said that although there were black supervisors and managers, they did not have the same powers as white ones.

There was a strong commitment among top management (general managers, production managers and human resource managers) to all the components of the Equity programme. They realised that, because of the focus on salaried staff, the shop floor had tended to be neglected. While there was commitment to ensuring "human dignity" on the shop floor, the extension of affirmative action to people on the shop floor was not seen as a priority. It was recognised that if the focus was changed to cover more than the promotion of shop floor staff to supervisory positions, it would entail a number of changes that might be difficult at a time of a slower growth in profits. For example, if shop floor staff were to be recruited for salaried posts, existing staff would have to be scanned for potential and given intensive appropriate training. People being recruited for shop floor jobs in future would have to meet higher minimum requirements than in the past. Greater attention would have to be paid to training supervisors in the recognition of talent amongst their staff. The union and shop floor workers generally would need to be consulted in a more comprehensive way. Senior human resource staff do not see this as a problem.

CONSULTATION WITH BLACK STAFF

African salaried staff who were interviewed had some contrasting things to say about whether they should have a voice in the development and implementation of the Equity policy. One manager who had once been a union

---

1. *Urin Ferndale,* Equity in SAB Beer Division, *SAB internal document, 25 January 1994.*

organiser did not think that a forum or task group of "Equity beneficiaries" would be a good idea. He dismissed the idea of creating a "solidarity forum" to protect employees as counter-productive because it went against the principles of performance management. In terms of these, every person was part of a multi-disciplinary work team and was responsible for his or her own "self-management and performance". Another black manager said that he also did not think there ought to be a forum or pressure group of black managerial staff:

> It goes against performance management principles ... We are not a working
> team in the sense that we are working on a specific task together ... It would be
> like a caucus group and it might promote racial tensions. We need to have
> confidence in ourselves as people so that I have the guts to go to my manager
> and say that he is not being fair.

On the other hand, a third African manager said:

> Having an affirmative action policy is something that is going to determine my
> movement in a company or my stay in a company. But nobody bothered to
> discuss it with me. So, to me, it is like the same old thing: 'We know what's good
> for them.'

He pointed out that this was common to most companies "that like to say to you, 'we are very liberal', instead of saying, 'listen, we are in the process of changing and we want you to help us'. What they are saying is, 'we have nothing to learn'."

There was some discussion among both those in human resources and higher management and among black salaried staff about how the latter could be more involved in policy-making in affirmative action. However, something similar was tried in the past and found unsatisfactory.

The Alrode plant has a forum on Equity for black salaried staff, which is chaired by the general manager. It meets about every six months and there is open discussion. There is also some informal mentoring among black staff.

LINE RATHER THAN STAFF POSITIONS FOR BLACKS

It was forcibly put to me that whites would only be convinced that blacks could do the job as well as they could once a black occupied a line position. If blacks were confined to the "soft" disciplines of industrial relations and human resources, they would cut no ice as decision-makers with responsibility for the "bottom line". This interviewee was quick to point out that he would not like to find himself with insufficient preparation for such responsibility. He said it was essential that blacks be put into jobs where their capacity could be measured against the toughest standards. Of course, there were blacks in line positions at SAB, but they were fewer in number than those in staff functions.

At the SAB central office, positions held by both blacks and whites carried the title of "personal assistant" (PA). These posts were attached to executive directors (who were all white up to July, 1994 when the first black director was appointed) who were responsible for training their PAs. Black managers at the central office with whom I discussed this were highly critical of these positions because blacks were seen as being assistants to whites. To them, they failed to offer blacks the opportunity to make decisions that counted. The view commonly held by blacks interviewed was that the PA was confined to making recommendations that, if they were good, would be credited to the incumbent of the "real" position. If they were bad, they would be blamed on the PA.

Another reason why there should be more black line managers is that there is a "buffer zone" of white middle managers who are often conservative or fearful for their own futures and who frustrate company progress. Shop stewards said they were blocking agreements that had been negotiated and agreed between union and management. In their view it would be better if this stratum had more blacks, whom they imagined would be more sympathetic to the union. The shop stewards also said that if this layer of management was included in the negotiations, they would feel that they had shared in the agreements reached and would thus be less likely to frustrate them. Top management, on the other hand, recognised that it is these conservative, white middle managers who most feared and disliked Equity. They often tried to frustrate its aims and had a negative effect on the company's industrial relations at plant level.

Successful black line managers argued that blacks needed to be more determined and more strategic in their career planning than at present. They had to be prepared to make sacrifices in order to get the experience and training that they needed for line management positions. One particularly successful manager saw that the only job to which he could be promoted in the human resources field was that of national human resources director. The incumbent, however, was quite young and unlikely to move soon:

> I decided to lose my status and become a production trainee so that I would
> have a future in general management. I trained in packaging. For a whole year I
> was a trainee, working shifts and wearing overalls. (Interview with general
> manager.)

Too few blacks, he argued, were prepared to get their hands dirty and forego their high status positions in order to better position themselves for advancement.

Finally, in looking at the pyramidal structure of the organisation and the levels which black salaried staff have reached, it seems that there could be a block for blacks to surmount between the SAB "G" grade (equivalent to Paterson C 1 – 3) and the higher "H" grade (Paterson C 4 – 5). Employees in Grade H and above have traditionally been recruited from outside as graduates and put through internal management training. This is how current black incumbents of those grades have achieved them. Unless employees in the lower grades are put through degrees at company expense or degrees are dropped as essential qualifications for top posts, it will be difficult for people from the shop floor to move into management.

OVERLOOKING INSIDE TALENT AND POTENTIAL

The Equity survey of late 1993 showed that "blacks are frustrated by the fact that blacks from outside the company are appointed in senior positions instead of promoting employees from within". This perception persists despite the fact that it is not true and that all vacancies are first advertised and filled, where possible, within company ranks.

Even those blacks who have been recruited as graduates complained that they were overlooked for promotion. One of the managers I interviewed had been an employee at SAB, resigned in frustration at his lack of progress and then returned at a much higher level after quite a short absence. His view was that he would not have reached his present level at SAB unless he had left and come back. "You become part of the furniture," he said, and are overlooked in favour of talent recruited from outside. Even supervisors, it was claimed, were frequently chosen from outside rather than by grooming internal potential. Leaving and returning to a higher position had happened to whites, but was much more noted and resented when it happened to blacks.

The extent to which there was a concerted effort to recruit talent from the shop floor to overseer or supervisor varied from plant to plant. However, it appeared to be quite difficult to be promoted from these posts into higher levels of management. Further, efforts to recruit from the shop floor into artisan or other training opportunities provided by the company have not been successful. A number of managers told me that they were constantly looking for talent. Black managers and shop stewards said that, although there were many shop floor workers with Std 9 and matric, they were not being advanced in any way.

This failure to recruit internally caused frustration among well-qualified shop floor and supervisory staff. It was also recognised that if the company was going to scout for talent in, and recruit from, the lower grades, it would have to develop higher level criteria for appointment to the shop floor and be willing to pay its workers more.

Part of the problem here might lie in the fact that the training and recruitment divisions in at least one of the breweries are separate sections of the human resources departments. At this site, training is responsible for the assessment of people's potential and not recruitment. People are therefore not assessed for their potential when they are recruited to the shop floor. (Interview, personnel officer.)

Several black interviewees questioned the validity of the psychometric tests that were used to assess potential. They were suspicious of the content: "Why should I be expected to know the rivers of England?" asked one puzzled shop steward who had applied for promotion. "How is it relevant to the job here?"

Tests were evaluated by correlating test results with subsequent job performance, but this was not happening at some of the sites studied, where they appeared to be used as a swift and efficient filtering mechanism.

On the other hand, the main driver for promotion was not so much testing or even training, but career path discussions that were supposed to take place under the Equity programme with every single employee. This ambitious plan has yet to reach all shop floor staff, though it did appear to be working well at salaried and managerial levels. What black managers in the production plants valued, especially those with experience as "affirmative action appointees" in other organisations, was that they were given real jobs to do, with real responsibilities.

CONCLUSION

SAB Beer Division has been taking action with a view to increasing the number of Africans, Asians and coloureds on its salaried staff for more than two decades. The company has done so in a number of clear phases, marked by changes in both written and effective policy procedures. Each phase has been embarked upon deliberately as the result of a careful assessment of the successes and failures of previous policy. The endeavour has, on each occasion, not been driven by changes in the business climate, which has remained consistently positive for SAB in the beer market. Instead, it has been driven by the personal commitment of highly placed and influential individuals – the chief executive advised and assisted by the human resources director.

The policies have been successful in coming extremely close to the original target of 50 percent of all salaried staff. The actual figure is 48 percent. However, the latest phase recognises that the spread of black people up the hierarchy and across from the "soft" into the "hard" disciplines is not satisfactory. Nor is the record on the recruitment and promotion of women of all races. The most recent policy makes provision for this spread to be achieved. The policy with respect to women has not been spelled out and where women are being accorded greater attention it is as a result of individual managers' initiatives.

Affirmative action has been granted high status in the company: it ranks as one of the five major business objectives. As a result, there is now strong pressure on individual managers to set ambitious targets and to meet them. This has occasionally been done with a loss of efficiency, and incompetent black managers have been advised that they should seek alternative employment. There is a determination among top managers that targets should be achieved without loss of efficiency and with due regard for the merit principle. It is accepted that this may mean longer than ideal lead times between the decision that a particular position should be occupied by a black person and a suitable incumbent being trained and gaining the necessary experience. There is thus considerable emphasis on personal career planning and appropriate training.

At the head office there appears to be considerable discontent among black salaried staff, particularly, that they were being overlooked in favour of new black appointees from outside. However, contrary to what one might expect at a firm as committed as this one to affirmative action for blacks, there was not obvious unhappiness among whites. It may be that those who had found it unacceptable have left. The atmosphere at the production sites visited was remarkable: people appeared to be satisfied with their jobs and their progress and pleased to be working hard in a challenging environment. ■

INTERESTS AND HOLDINGS OF THE SOUTH AFRICAN BREWERIES GROUP

BEER AND COMPLEMENTARY BEVERAGES

1. SAB Beer Division   100%
      70% of United Breweries (Pty) Ltd
      70% of Ohlsson's Brewery Transkei (Pty) Ltd
      55% of Southern Associated Maltsters (Pty) Ltd
      100% of SAB Hop Farms (Pty) Ltd

2. Westgate Worldwide Inc   100%
      100% of Indol International BV
      83% of Compania Cervecera da Canaris SA
      100% of Appletise Plc

3. Amalgamated Beverage Industries Ltd   68%
      24% of Amalgamated Beverage Canners (Pty) Ltd

4. Appletiser South Africa (Pty) Ltd   100%
      35% of Ceres Fruit Juices (Pty) Ltd
      75% of Valaqua (Pty) Ltd

5. Traditional Beer Investments   100%
      50% of Bophutatswana Breweries (Pty) Ltd

6. Distillers Corporation (SA) Ltd   30%

7. Stellenbosch Farmers Winery Group Ltd   30%

RETAIL AND HOTELS

1. OK Bazaars (1929) Ltd   69%

2. Amalgamated Retail Ltd   69%
      76% of Boymans Ltd

3. Edgars Stores Ltd   65%

4. Southern Sun Holdings Ltd   100%
        50% of Southern Sun Leisure Investments
        45% of Hotel Formule 1 (Pty) Ltd
        27% of Nedtravel (Pty) Ltd
        20% of Sun International Inc

MANUFACTURING

1. Associated Furniture Companies Ltd   66%
        50% of Kallenbach-Hendler (Pty) Ltd
        50% of Resinkem (Pty) Ltd
        21% of Romatex Ltd

2. The Lion Match Company Ltd   71%
        50% of Amalgamated Appliances (Pty) Ltd

3. Da Gama Textile Company Ltd   61%

4. Plate Glass and Shatterprufe Industries Ltd   68%
        100% of Glass South Africa (Pty) Ltd
        72% of PG Bison Ltd
        85% of Belron International NV
        45% of PG Industries Zimbabwe Ltd
        32% of Pilkington Glass (Zimbabwe) (Pty) Ltd

5. Conshu Holdings Ltd   33%

Source: South African Breweries Group Annual Report 1993

TRAINING

Bursars are sponsored at universities and technikons on a contract basis, which requires students to work for SAB for one year for each year of sponsored study.

In 1993, blacks comprised 62 percent of a total of 52 bursars. In 1994, they made up 65 percent of a total of 50. The success rate in obtaining permanent posts with SAB after the end of the contractual period was low but they were attempting to improve this. Figures have been kept centrally only since early 1993. Of the 13 who graduated and completed their contract period in 1993, six were appointed to permanent posts. The figure for 1994 is 11 out of 13.

DEVELOPMENT BANK OF

SOUTHERN AFRICA

NAJWAH ALLIE-EDRIES

PROFILE OF THE COMPANY

The Development Bank of Southern Africa (DBSA) was established in 1983 after a multilateral agreement was reached between the former homeland states and South Africa. The latter holds 84 percent of the equity and two-thirds of the voting power. After the democratic elections in April 1994, the South African government became the sole shareholder. DBSA is controlled by a council of governors and a board of directors to which the chief executive reports.

DBSA was established within the context of apartheid planning. It primarily serviced the development needs of the former homelands and self-governing territories. It was perceived to be an institution of the apartheid government, which was able to exert control over the bank through prescribing its mandate. This meant that the bank could only fund development projects that fell within the parameters set by government.

As with all government institutions, the bank was characterised by a bureaucratic organisational structure and dominated by white, Afrikaner males, a legacy that the bank is still trying to shed. The release of Nelson Mandela and the political developments that followed heralded a new phase in South African politics, and the management of DBSA decided to restructure the organisation and implement affirmative action more actively than it had done before.

DBSA's core business activity is to finance development. It does this by providing loan finance and technical assistance at concessionary rates. DBSA's major clients were the governments of the former TBVC (Transkei, Bophuthatswana, Venda and Ciskei) states and self-governing territories. Other clients include non-governmental organisations (NGOs) and local municipalities. The bank sees itself as a "wholesaler" of development resources. It does not implement projects but funds and supports intermediaries who implement the projects in conjunction with targeted communities. The bank also renders services in policy formulation and programming and development planning support is also provided to the relevant institutions at central, regional and local level.

The organisation is divided into an operations division and support services. The operations division in turn is divided into four geographic regions and each region consists of a multi-disciplinary team of specialists and project leaders who work exclusively on development projects in their designated region. Support services cover policy and information analysis, finance, corporate management services and corporate affairs.

As at March 1994, the DBSA employed 575 employees, of which 3 percent were Asian, 31 percent African, 1 percent coloured and 65 percent white. (See table overleaf.) This was a change from the almost all-white employee profile when the bank was established. This case study will attempt to explain the process and reasons for these changes at DBSA.

South Africa's socio-economic environment has encouraged a proliferation of development agencies. At present no state department or private institution co-ordinates development assistance. Active in the development arena are government departments, provincial administrations, state-sponsored corporations such as the Independent Development Trust and DBSA and a wide range of NGOs.

Because development and reconstruction are high on the political agenda, development agencies have been thrust into the political spotlight. Intensive debate on the role, relevance, sources of finance and future co-ordination of development agencies has ensued. As international donors reassess their funding criteria, most organisations have had to reassess their objectives.

The outgoing chief executive of the DBSA has said that the debate should not focus on the survival of the bank per se, but rather on the survival of the functions entrusted to it. The management and staff of DBSA generally believe that the organisation has an important role to play in the development of the southern Africa region.

Historically, the bank has been able to nurture critical skills and expertise. International development agencies are starting to enter South Africa and DBSA believes that it will be able to provide the local experience and expertise needed to balance development initiatives.

DBSA's management recognises that if the bank is to remain relevant in a changed South Africa, it will have to change its employment practices, structure and operational strategy. Under pressure from political change and economic realities, the management of DBSA took the decision to embark on a process of internal transformation. This process was facilitated by a change in the mindset of a few managers and staff who believed that the bank had to become more proactive in its approach, not only to development initiatives, but also in terms of its employment policies.

◼ TABLE 1 ◼

PERMANENT STAFF STRENGTH BY RACE, GENDER AND SKILL LEVEL. MARCH 31, 1994

PATERSON GRADE	WHITE	BLACK	COLOURED	ASIAN	TOTAL	WOMEN
NON-EXEC DIR						
F	5				5	
E 4-5	2				2	
E 1-3	15	2			17	1
D 4-5	141	16	1		158	19
D 1-3	84	22		4	110	23
C 4-5	32	33	2	6	73	37
C 1-3	82	25	2	3	112	88
B	16	48	1	3	68	40
A		30			30	17
UNGRADED						
TOTAL	377	176	6	16	575	225

Source: UCT Graduate School of Business — Breakwater Monitor
Notes:
Paterson F   Executive Directors
Paterson E 4-5   Senior — Executive Management
Paterson E 1-3   Senior Management
Paterson D 4-5   Middle — Senior Management
Paterson D 1-3   Junior — Middle Management
Paterson C 4-5   Assistant Management — Senior Supervisory & Junior Professional
Paterson C 1-3   Graduate Entry, Supervisory, Artisan & Technician, Senior Operative
                      & Senior Admin/Clerical/Secretarial
Paterson B   Operative, Admin/Clerical/Secretarial
Paterson A   Entry Level Operative & Labourer

METHOD AND SAMPLE

Approximately 25 interviews were conducted at DBSA between December 1993 and January 1994. Interviewees were selected to provide a cross-section of the staff employed at the bank. These were supplemented with informal discussions with individuals and interest groups.

The distribution of interviews was as follows:

	BLACK		WHITE		
	MEN	WOMEN	MEN	WOMEN	TOTAL
MANAGERS	2	2	4	1	9
PROFESSIONALS	3	3	3	1	10
SUPPORT STAFF	2	2	1	1	6
TOTAL	7	7	8	3	25

■ TABLE 2 ■

HISTORY OF AFFIRMATIVE ACTION

Political changes, together with changes in approach to development strategy, accelerated the transformation process within the bank. DBSA had to become more responsive to its clients who felt that the bank took a long time to respond to the needs of communities. The bank also had to change from an Afrikaner male-dominated bureaucratic organisation to a racially representative, flexible and responsive institution. In 1990, only one black male was employed in a senior management position. Black staff were employed primarily in lower-level positions. This was despite the bank's Articles of Agreement that stipulated that the composition of staff had to reflect the demography of South Africa.

Many explanations were given for the absence of blacks among senior employees. It was clear that at the time the recruitment of blacks was not a priority for the white, Afrikaner, male managers and there was no pressure on them to change. Another explanation was that it was unacceptable for blacks to work at the bank because it was perceived to be an institution of the apartheid government. One of the black interviewees said that he would not have taken a job there in the past.

The information that follows documents the changes in staff policy that have taken place at DBSA over the years. These changes eventually culminated in the formulation and adoption of a formal affirmative action policy.

EMPLOYMENT EQUITY

DBSA has always been influenced by changes in the external political environment. While it has at times been proactive in readjusting its development focus, it has not always been proactive in its staffing policies. As a consequence, changes in staffing policy were mainly the result of external pressures. This meant, in effect, that management responded with whatever policies it thought were appropriate at the time.

In May 1989, DBSA management identified employment equity as a strategic objective and released a document entitled *DBSA 2000*, which included the following vision statement:

> The bank firmly believes that our staff composition should increasingly reflect the composition of the total population of southern Africa.

Various strategies and procedures have been initiated to implement this vision. For example, the recruitment policy began to target black staff at entry levels, such as secretaries, administrative staff and young professionals. The manager of corporate affairs at the time, Dr Jannie Zaaiman, said: "We began by targeting our professionals and secretaries. The feeling was that we would have the most visible success in these areas."

By November 1993, black secretarial staff made up 64 percent of the total number of secretaries employed. While there had been an increase in the number of black professional staff, this occurred primarily at the lower levels. Top management continued to be dominated by white, Afrikaner males. Alongside its recruitment strategy, the bank management also attempted to make a more concerted effort to identify blacks within the organisation who could benefit from further training. Management did not commit itself to saying that this was training for management positions, but rather that it had to be viewed as part of general staff development.

In 1990, in response to *DBSA 2000*, the Urban Development Group, a division within the bank, decided to develop its own approach to staff development. The group saw itself as a sample that could be used to develop pilot policies. If these were successful they could be applied to the whole of DBSA. A questionnaire was devised to assess the staff situation within the Urban Development Group and to test areas of concern about staff enhancement and identify other issues. The main findings were:

- Within the group there were opinions and attitudes about the staff complement that were not conducive to a change from the status quo.
- No significant changes in the racial and gender compositions of staff had been implemented.

The report found:

> The organisation has a number of espoused policies and principles. However they do not appear to have been translated into effective actions or to have resulted in any significant changes in approach.

It also noted that to increase the employment of women at all levels of the organisation, specific policies for the advancement of women had to be created.

By 1991, management recognised that changes in the external environment meant that the absence of black staff and women at senior, professional and managerial levels would have to be addressed as a priority. To make the bank more representative of the communities it served, the board issued a directive that by the end of 1993 at least 30 percent of staff should be made up of blacks and women. Management agreed that the emphasis should be on the quality of staff and that they should not merely play a numbers game.

AFFIRMATIVE ACTION

In 1992, a new document outlining DBSA's human resources management and development strategies for 1992/1993 was approved by the executive committee. This document supported the vision outlined in *DBSA 2000* and provided background information and motivation for the plan proposed to implement employment equity.

The plan was formulated by senior management and it was decided that it should be implemented by a steering committee, consisting mainly of managers. This committee would be given decision-making powers and would be responsible for implementing employment equity at DBSA. The steering committee would have to address issues such as enhancing contact between different levels of staff, bridging cultural differences and breaking down stereotypes. It would also have to examine the issue of sensitising staff to the changed mindsets, values and culture necessary to take the organisation forward. In essence, management believed that it was necessary to establish understanding and co-ownership for the employment equity process among all bank employees. The steering committee would also co-ordinate the implementation of actions by the human resources team and other identified parties.

Management also decided to appoint an outside consultant to assist the steering committee with the management of employment equity in the bank. The consultant was asked to comment on the actions of the steering committee and monitor the progress made against the strategic goals that had been set. The bank's management also said that an Affirmative Action Co-ordinating Committee (AACC) should be democratically elected consisting of staff representatives from all divisions. It would be used by the steering committee as a sounding board to test ideas and to obtain feedback before implementing any decisions.

Members of staff interviewed said that people were encouraged in an ad hoc manner to come up with ideas about what affirmative action should mean for the bank and how such a policy could be made to work. This request was met with a mixed response. A few employees submitted ideas to the AACC or to the human resources department or wrote to *Debansa*, the internal newsletter, while others merely observed the process.

The initial affirmative action committee consisted of two representatives from each department, altogether a total of 22 members. The committee was later reduced to seven because it was felt that a smaller committee could be more effective. The activities of the AACC are outlined in detail below. Other than the establishment of the AACC, there was no articulated strategy to systematically involve all role players in the process of policy formulation.

Senior managers envisaged that the AACC would report to the steering committee because they felt that the latter would be the guardian of affirmative action within the bank. The AACC, however, requested the chief executive to review his functions/role in this regard. It was felt that the basic premise of the affirmative action initiative was to encourage staff participation in affirmative action interventions, and therefore it would be important to have direct access to the chief executive. If he openly endorsed the initiative, the process would be more credible. A member of the AACC said: "The bottom-up approach needed a top-down commitment". The chief executive accepted this and the steering committee disbanded.

THE AFFIRMATIVE ACTION CO-ORDINATING COMMITTEE

In 1993, the 22 committee members were elected by their respective divisions. However, interviews revealed that not all staff members were satisfied with the representatives elected. Various other interest groups, such as the Women's Forum and the Staff Association, were also part of the affirmative action team as they acted as watchdogs for their constituencies.

The AACC has no delegated authority. It advises the chief executive, tries to influence staff thinking about affirmative action issues and acts as a watchdog. The AACC has no separate operating budget and members of the committee had different views on the issue. Some felt that there had been no difficulty accessing funds and that, therefore, it did not need to have its own budget. Others felt that by having its own budget, the AACC could be seen to be truly independent of management. A few AACC members argued that the chief executive had been visible in his commitment to affirmative action and had not hesitated to make funds available to be used at the AACC's discretion. For example, funds were requested to buy teaching resources, host workshops and to attend relevant conferences.

On the question of a separate budget, the chief executive said: "I have requested the AACC to submit a budget, but I think that in providing for affirmative action through the normal operating budget of the bank it becomes more integrated with the operational ethic of the organisation."

The AACC considered the appointment of a full-time person to drive the affirmative action initiative because it was felt that the committee members could not devote sufficient time to the project. No decision had been reached by the time this research was concluded.

The AACC has no formal procedural rules and, to some extent, this affects the work rate of some of the members. They have not always been able to complete their tasks on time. It was accepted, however, that members took on affirmative action activities in addition to their normal work-related activities.

Thus while the AACC identified a few priority tasks, it did not develop a strategic plan of operation. In fact, there appeared to be no long-term vision of the future role of the committee, whether it would continue in its present form or play a much reduced role in the future.

The AACC saw as its first task the identification of issues to be addressed in the short term, such as the bank's performance in terms of its stated recruitment objective. It also wanted to investigate the policy alternatives for affirmative action at DBSA. The AACC divided its members into a number of teams that were asked to investigate the various policy options and each team had to submit an action plan to the AACC. The teams covered areas such as promotions and rewards, performance appraisal, training and development, recruitment, consultants, sensitising and dissemination. These action plans identified the key issues of concern, suggested a way of dealing with the problem and set target dates.

The investigations culminated in a two-day workshop for the AACC, members of the human resources department and the manager who had participated in the process. The purpose of the workshop was to develop specific recommendations for the implementation of affirmative action at the bank.

The report that flowed from this workshop was known as the *Aloe Ridge Report, November 1992* and it defined what DBSA meant by affirmative action:

> Affirmative action consists of a process to design and implement interventions
> that focus on the correction of historical and current imbalances and the
> maximising of the potential of staff members.

The report also contained recommendations on issues such as recruitment and selection, performance appraisal, training and development and rewards and promotions.

RECRUITMENT AND SELECTION

The policy adopted was intended to ensure that the most appropriate candidates were recruited and selected at all levels with special preference being given to the previously disadvantaged. The policy statement was supported by guidelines. For example, selection criteria had to emphasise the potential to develop and recruitment and selection decisions had to be supported by deliberate training interventions and personal support. In this way the performance barriers that were caused by culture, attitude and values could be removed. All vacancies from normal labour turnover would be available for affirmative action appointees.

Recruitment officers also had to show that, for any particular skill required, every attempt was made to recruit from disadvantaged groups. Strong motivations for recruiting from any other group were necessary. Details on recruitment procedures were also outlined in the report. For example, internal recruitment from disadvantaged groups would always be the first option. The report also recommended that the interview panel be extended, according to the demands of the specific position, to include peers and a representative of the AACC. Existing job grades were not to be used as screening criteria and selection criteria for all vacancies had to facilitate affirmative action. Specific regard had to be given to candidates' degrees of experience.

STAFF APPRAISAL

The report recommended that DBSA adopt an appraisal policy that was objective, transparent and fully supportive of affirmative action by taking into consideration both staff performance and potential for development. The policy statement was supported by guidelines stating that individuals were to be fully informed at all times about how they were performing. Standardised performance criteria were applied to all staff, and subordinate and peer appraisal of managers was made a part of the appraisal system. The policy statement also provided for an AACC representative on the human resources committee. There were also incentives for managers who promoted staff development, complied with affirmative action and ensured full transparency of all staff appraisals.

TRAINING AND DEVELOPMENT

The policy objective of the report was to give all individuals the opportunity to maximise their potential but with special emphasis on candidates from the previously disadvantaged groups. Policy guidelines specified that affirmative action candidates with special potential be identified, notified and given the opportunity of accelerated development. All affirmative action candidates also had to have career plans that could guide further personal development. One of the procedures outlined was that each manager had to identify a candidate/s for management development. A specific development plan had to be drawn up in consultation with the human resources department and the candidate. The development plan would include specific objectives and time frames.

REWARDS AND PROMOTIONS

The report recommended a promotions policy that would move identified people into appropriate positions based on their demonstrated competence, while taking into account historical and current imbalances. The guidelines said that there should be equal access to promotion and that all grading inconsistencies should be addressed and gaps narrowed. It was also recommended that the 10 percent promotion quota be applied primarily to black candidates. The current promotion forms should be revised to include an affirmative action focus. Furthermore, all applicants whose promotions were rejected must be provided with reasons.

The employment equity policies already in operation had to be reviewed to ensure that they supported the new approach. Once all policies had been brought into line and approved by the workshop participants, the policy document would be made available to all employees. The chief executive would be responsible for communicating the bank's affirmative action policy to the organisation.

To assist the process of implementation, the chief executive and the general managers held a workshop at which they tried to assimilate the strategic implications of affirmative action for DBSA. In addition, the directors, general managers and divisional managers also attended a workshop at which they attempted to integrate the affirmative action recommendations into the organisation's operational guidelines. The AACC was represented at both workshops. Sensitising workshops were held for middle management and senior specialists and it was hoped that all staff would have the opportunity to attend these workshops. This had not happened by the time this research was completed and interviews revealed that staff below management level were not aware of them.

Members of the human resources division said that they were not driving the affirmative action initiative, but that they were working with the AACC in rewriting the relevant policies. Interviews also revealed that at first the relationship between the two had been strained and characterised by mistrust as rules had not been clearly defined. For example, the AACC believed that the human resources division had not done enough to implement affirmative action over the years while the human resources division believed that the AACC was trying to take over its functions and become involved in an area in which it had no expertise. Since then the relationship has improved. Those interviewed said this was because tasks, functions and responsibilities had now been clearly defined.

In addition to the guidelines and procedures, there were specific monitoring actions and clear roles and responsibilities for all role-players. The completion of the policy document in October 1993 was the result of more collaboration between human resources staff and the AACC. This document was essentially a refinement of the *Aloe Ridge Report*, which was never recognised as official DBSA policy.

By November 1993, the affirmative action policy document was endorsed by the chief executive. This new document covered all the same strategic issues as the previous document. More importantly, all new role-players were given the opportunity to discuss and amend the policy. In this way they were encouraged to take ownership of the affirmative action programme.

RECESSION, RESTRUCTURING AND AFFIRMATIVE ACTION

In 1993, while the different role players were trying to identify their role in the affirmative action programme, DBSA management launched an internal restructuring exercise. The AACC was not consulted; a member of the AACC said: "Management was very clear on this issue. They told us that this action was management's prerogative." The management said that it was "right sizing" – ensuring that the organisation had the correct staff complement to ensure optimal efficiency. Management claimed that the need to make use of the staff's potential more efficiently was an added motivation for the restructuring exercise.

Restructuring entailed dividing the operations division into four geographic "regions". Staff were assigned to each region to create a multidisciplinary team. The teams consisted of a number of different divisions, including: rural and urban development; infrastructure; institutional development; business and entrepreneurial development; and development planning and human resources development. Each region was also assigned a number of specialists: financial; technical; people participation; environmental; etc. As part of the process, the managerial hierarchy was flattened, reducing it to one level of management.

Restructuring was not accompanied by large-scale retrenchments; at the time, only 10 employees left the organisation because they could not be accommodated in the new structure or because they were not satisfied with the restructuring exercise. The impact of the restructuring exercise on the affirmative action programme was uneven. A member of the AACC said:

> The restructuring process allowed for the opening up of the management echelon and provided people with potential to be identified and promoted. Of concern to the AACC, however, is that even though the bank has appointed some blacks in top management positions, not enough of the appointments have been as a result of internal promotions.

The staff at DBSA were bombarded with change from all directions. Externally their client base began to change. Internally they had to deal with a different organisational structure, a different management structure, new faces, new policies and new committees. Interviews reveal that people within DBSA responded very differently to all these changes. Some people took refuge in their work, shutting out the changes. Others welcomed the changes. There were some who were disillusioned, but this was never expressed in open opposition. The following response probably sums up a common feeling among employers: "Why rock the boat, DBSA takes good care of my children's education."

The organisational changes that occurred at the time slowed down the implementation of affirmative action. Employees and management could not give due attention to it. The appointment of a new human resources general manager also necessitated introducing him and his staff to the policy guidelines. Another workshop was held after which a reworked and more refined affirmative action policy document was developed, and the definition of affirmative action was refined:

> Affirmative action refers to interventions to redress historical and current discrimination and imbalances whereafter employment equity practices are to be put in place.

Employees interviewed agreed that the restructuring process had indeed assisted the bank to speed up its response to its clients. While the restructuring process slowed down the implementation of affirmative action, the result was not entirely negative since it created employment opportunities for affirmative action candidates.

EVALUATION OF THE POLICY

COMMUNICATING AFFIRMATIVE ACTION

The AACC liaised directly with the chief executive, who in turn communicated affirmative action policy to his general managers who reported to their respective divisional managers. Representatives on the AACC were responsible for reporting to their constituencies and the AACC was also represented on the human resources committee, which was a forum of general managers.

The verbal communication system was, however, not supported by a well defined written communication system. Nor did the AACC implement formal channels for the communication of affirmative action policy. The result was that, since not all AACC representatives reported to their constituencies, the information flow on affirmative action policy was uneven. This also meant that because the activities or achievements of the AACC were not regularly documented, staff tended to think that it was just another committee. This type of attitude detracted from the credibility of the work of the committee.

The absence of regular, formal communication also gave rise to speculation that management was not committed to the implementation of affirmative action. A number of people interviewed thought that managers were only paying lip service to affirmative action. They said management merely wanted to be seen to be saying the right things, but were not really committed to the programme. As a result, the interviewees felt that a manager's performance appraisal should be rated against his/her implementation of affirmative action. A few AACC representatives said that because some general managers and divisional managers were not committed to affirmative action it was difficult to have proper reportbacks on AACC activities. It was also difficult to initiate activities that would facilitate the acceptance of affirmative action within the organisation.

The lack of communication caused some uncertainty among white employees and some black employees, especially those in the lower ranks, felt that the benefits of affirmative action did not apply to them anyway.

SPREAD OF ROLES AND RESPONSIBILITY

The extent to which the affirmative action initiative at DBSA has been successful is partially because the responsibility for designing and implementing affirmative action is spread among a wide range of individuals and groups within the bank. For example, the commitment of the chief executive lends credibility to the policy and encourages the broader organisation to accept the process. The AACC monitors the implementation, but also makes recommendations directly to the chief executive. The human resources department assists with the writing of policy and is also responsible for implementation. Implementation of affirmative action is also the responsibility of general managers and divisional managers.

The spread of responsibility has also had a positive impact on the image of the AACC because it was prevented from becoming a lobbying group which could have had a negative impact on its relationship with management. A situation could have developed where management viewed the AACC as the "enemy".

RECRUITMENT AND SELECTION

The AACC has told management:

> The committee believes that recruitment inside the bank has not been vigorous enough and feels strongly that affirmative action begins at home and that internal opportunities should be opened up for upward mobility.

One manager's response to this was that it was very difficult to find suitably qualified black staff, but it was also said that management could be guilty of not looking hard enough, or in the right places. It was also felt by those interviewed that not enough internal grooming was being done in terms of succession planning. No proactive training and development were taking place.

Of those interviewed, management and staff alike cited the bank's recruitment of blacks as one of its major successes. Between April 1992 and April 1994, the bank recruited a total of 81 employees, 63 percent of whom were black. The bank recruits by word of mouth and staff are encouraged to identify appropriate candidates either internally or externally. DBSA does not advertise posts outside the bank, and employees are always given first option for any new vacancies. If a suitable candidate cannot be found in the bank, external recruitment is allowed but managers are warned that affirmative action principles must apply. If this condition cannot be satisfied, a strong motivation must accompany the appointment.

Of the total number of people interviewed during 1992, 68 percent were from the affirmative action target group. In 1993 this figure increased to 79 percent. Of the total number of people appointed in 1992, 70 percent were from the affirmative action target group, while the corresponding figure for 1993 was 72 percent. As a result, the bank achieved its 1993 target of 30 percent.

When asked whether all blacks recruited were affirmative action candidates, a member of management staff said that the bank recruited from a constituency which it had identified as needing affirmative action. Once recruited all employees were regarded as equal. The question arose as it became apparent, during the interviewing process, that the term "affirmative action candidate" carried many negative connotations. Black people resented this labelling and insisted that they occupied positions within the bank by virtue of the qualifications they already possessed.

Despite achieving the 1993 target of 30 percent, some of those interviewed still questioned whether the new appointments had any real authority. They asked whether these jobs had real decision-making powers and were critical positions within the bank's hierarchy.

RETENTION OF BLACK EMPLOYEES

While DBSA management claimed that the organisation had been successful in recruiting blacks, this must be seen against the background of both whites and blacks leaving the organisation. Of the total number of new recruits, nine had already left the organisation by the time this study was completed. They comprised six Africans, three males and three females; one Asian male; one white male; and one white female. Exit interviews revealed that people had left for the following reasons:

Comments from some white employees:

The organisation favours blacks.

There is uncertainty about jobs, about the future of the bank.

Comments from some black employees:

In theory everything is in place; in practice the bank has a long way to go. Racism still exists, the bank is still far from achieving parity.

I could not resist the job offer.

Affirmative action at the bank is not effective, the bank does not fully utilise internal skills.

Some people left the organisation because they could not cope with the internal changes. Others left because they felt the organisation was not really committed to the policies it espoused. There were those who left because they had a personal history of disagreement with staff at the bank. Not all of those who left felt negative about the future of the organisation, and most of those who left had better job offers.

Between September 1993 and April 1994, 29 black employees were appointed, 15 females and 14 males. Of those appointed, only 17 percent, or five people, were appointed above the Paterson Grade D2 lower level and they were all male. During the same period, 30 white employees were appointed, 16 females and 14 males. Of the 14 males appointed, 57 percent, or eight men, were appointed above the D2 lower level.

The affirmative action policy document stipulates that recruitment will be monitored on a quarterly basis. The AACC will do this with the assistance of the human resources division. In reviewing existing recruitment practices in the bank, the AACC recruitment task team reported that the current interviewing process was not satisfactory in that there was a lack of consistency. They recommended that the AACC should be allowed to intervene when people were shortlisted. A system of recourse should be put in place so that a final decision could be challenged.

SENSITISATION AND DISSEMINATION

Sensitisation is another area where the bank's management and the AACC have fallen short. Not enough has been done to interact with all the bank's employees on affirmative action issues. Only a few workshops had been organised to sensitise people to racist and sexist attitudes and the fears of those who feel threatened by affirmative action have not been addressed.

The chief executive said:

> If you derive security from your professional ability and can deliver what is required then you have a long stay in the bank. If you can't cope with change, then DBSA is not the organisation to be in.

The task team responsible for this function was drawing up a strategy to overcome this shortcoming. One option being investigated was to introduce Diversity Games to create more awareness about diversity and to demonstrate the positive effects of diversity. Plays and intercultural training were also being investigated and affirmative action sensitising workshops for all divisions were envisaged.

CONCLUSION

Interviews revealed that initially DBSA did not have a policy blueprint for the implementation of affirmative action. The only given was that the chief executive had committed himself to implementing it. Roles and responsibilities evolved and were affected by changes in both the internal and external environments. Furthermore, as the organisation moved along this road, the policy was adapted and changed as circumstances required. It was also apparent that the implementation of the policy did not always follow the route outlined in the policy document. Indeed, when comparing the progress made with some of the tasks the AACC set itself, one could conclude that not much had been achieved in terms of the number of priorities that were set. The AACC chairman said in response to this that it was not only the outcome that was important, but the process used to achieve the goals. This was especially important in an affirmative action programme as the success of the programme was very often determined by the extent to which the process was participative and consultative.

The importance of consultation cannot be over-emphasised. Consultation requires involving employees in designing affirmative action programmes and also provides an opportunity to understand and temper peoples' fears and expectations. At DBSA, management thought that the issue of consultation would be covered if a representative AACC was democratically elected. The case study, however, revealed that this was not sufficient. Formal communication channels were required as an important backup. Consultation also provided the opportunity to gain support for the affirmative action initiative. This commitment to the process was critical for the successful implementation of the programme. Interviews confirmed that where managers were not committed, implementation was hampered.

Consultation thus ensures that policies reflect concerns on the ground, issues are addressed before they become crises and fears and expectations are managed timeously. Affirmative action should be a part of the organisation's culture and values. The whole organisation must take ownership of the process. Strong leadership is, however, also important, as is an affirmative action strategy that is specific to the organisation.

While the issue of leadership in driving the affirmative action programme is important, it is clear that while the chief executive drove the process from the top, he alone could not ensure that it was successfully implemented. It was, in fact, the spread of responsibility between the chief executive, the AACC, the human resources department, the general and divisional managers and employees that made the process of implementation more manageable. The chief executive and the AACC monitored the process while the other role-players were responsible for implementation.

The study at DBSA provided another important lesson. No matter how comprehensive your policy, no matter how widely you have consulted, without specific action plans, your policy will continue to gather dust in your filing cabinet. Maybe this is as far as some companies are prepared to go. At DBSA, however, the affirmative action policy document contained detailed steps on how to go about implementing the priorities identified in the policy document. This is not to say that the process of implementation has been smooth. Insufficient consultation, lack of commitment by a few managers, undefined roles and responsibilities and an internal restructuring exercise restricted the implementation of the programme. It is important to note, though, that affirmative action is a process and that it is affected by both the internal organisational environment as well as the external environment.

One priority area that DBSA has had success with is recruitment. This success is due not only to the fact that there were pressures from the external environment, or that targets were set, or because the process of recruitment was closely monitored. It was also because of the willingness and commitment that some managers and employees invested in the process. The fact that a space was created where management's decisions could be questioned, also provided additional impetus.

Over the past four years, DBSA has been bombarded by both internal and external pressures to change. This case study reveals that the organisation has indeed taken up this challenge. The success achieved with internal restructuring and affirmative action demonstrates that with effort and support apartheid institutions can begin the process of transforming themselves. The process is not an easy one, extensive consultation is required and this, of course, has to be accompanied by detailed implementation and monitoring procedures. At DBSA the management and staff have all, in one way or another, contributed to the successes and the failures of the affirmative action programme. The organisation still has a long way to go; many of the burning issues have yet to be addressed, but the organisation has started on the road to change and will continue on this road. ■

UNILEVER (SA)

ANGUS BOWMAKER-FALCONER

PROFILE OF THE COMPANY

Unilever (SA) is part of Unilever PLC, one of the largest consumer goods manufacturing and marketing businesses in the world. It has head offices in London and Rotterdam with parallel UK and Dutch boards (Unilever PLC and Unilever NV), but is run as one business. Unilever is large (sales of £24 billion per year), diverse (product categories include foods, detergents, personal products and speciality chemicals) and successful (profit of over £2 billion in 1992).

The global structure is decentralised, allowing for independent decision making, with individual companies benefiting from international research and development and support services. Unilever's 500 individual operating companies are spread across 75 countries, employing more than 200 000 people. Unilever (SA) includes the five operating companies shown in the table.

■ TABLE 1 ■

UNILEVER (SA) OPERATING COMPANIES

COMPANY	PRODUCTS & SERVICES
LEVER BROTHERS	DETERGENTS, PERSONAL WASH, HOUSEHOLD CLEANERS
UNIFOODS	EDIBLE FATS, MARGARINES, COOKING OILS, CHEESE
OLA	ICE CREAM
ELIDA PONDS	PERSONAL PRODUCTS
HUDSON & KNIGHT	INDUSTRIAL FATS & OILS

LEVER BROTHERS (SA)

Lever Brothers is the largest of the Unilever operating companies and employs 2 430 people nationally. Lever Brothers manufactures and markets various leading brands in the detergents, personal wash and household cleaners markets, and has been a dominant player in South Africa for many years. The company has factories in Durban, where the head office is located, and Boksburg, which has one of the most technologically sophisticated plants in the world.

Unfolding political and socio-economic changes, coupled with the re-entry of South Africa into the international business arena, have created new challenges, described by the managing director as an "incredible double wave approaching us". The first wave he calls "operation catch up" which in essence requires moving from a high cost/low productivity operation to becoming a world class producer. The second wave is one faced by the bigger consumer manufacturers world-wide. Cheaper brands have improved in quality over the years and now offer better value for money. This requires the stronger brands to produce higher quality at better prices.

In summary, the challenge for Lever Brothers is to cut costs by becoming leaner, more effective and more flexible. Its strategy, guided by the Unilever global detergents strategy and taking into consideration the realities of the South African context, has three main thrusts:
- Investment in technology.
- Redefinition of work processes, including the flattening of organisational structures.
- Development and empowerment of its people.

METHOD AND SAMPLE

Lever Brothers was selected as the research site because it is the largest of the Unilever operating companies. There were also interesting developments in one of its departments, which presented an example of how organisational change, business innovation and the management of affirmative action are simultaneously addressed. The findings are, therefore, presented as a case study within a case study. The broader case study presents an overview of the Unilever approach to affirmative action, and the more focused case study deals with recent developments in the Lever Brothers marketing department. Discussion and conclusions cut across these two cases.

The sample, shown in the tables overleaf, represents a cross section of the company according to skill level, functional area, race and gender, although the sample is biased towards head office and the marketing department in particular. The participants were selected by the company. A total of 26 people were interviewed from three sites: Unilever head office (2), Lever Brothers' head office (15) and the Lever Brothers' Boksburg factory (9). Interviewees

■ TABLE 2 ■

INTERVIEWEES BY SKILL LEVEL

EXECUTIVE & SENIOR MANAGEMENT	6
MIDDLE MANAGEMENT	6
JUNIOR MANAGEMENT, MANAGEMENT TRAINEES	8
SUPERVISORY, SKILLED & SHOP FLOOR	6
TOTAL NUMBER OF MANAGERS	26 (72%)

■ TABLE 3 ■

INTERVIEWEES BY RACE AND GENDER

BLACK MANAGERS	5 (20%)
WOMEN MANAGERS	5 (20%)
WHITE MEN	10 (39%)
BLACK MEN	10 (39%)
WHITE WOMEN	5 (20%)
BLACK WOMEN	1 (4 %)

were drawn from the marketing department (10); production & technical department (6); finance (4); human resources (4); sales (1); and general management – the managing director (1). Eighteen out of the 26 people interviewed were at management levels and 20 were men.

HISTORY OF AFFIRMATIVE ACTION

ACI DEVELOPMENT PROGRAMME (1970 – 1985)

Unilever's affirmative action initiatives go back to the 1970's when the ACI (African, Coloured, Indian) development programme was put in place. The rationale for embarking on affirmative action was:
- A realisation that white management resources alone would not satisfy future resource needs.
- An understanding of the need to develop and utilise the full spectrum of resources available in South Africa.
- In anticipation of changing socio-political developments in South Africa. Progress during the 1970-1985 period was successful against set targets,

especially in respect of Asian numbers in management and supervisory positions.

BLACK MANAGEMENT DEVELOPMENT TASK FORCE (1985 – 1993)

In 1985, a decision was taken to change the focus from ACI to Africans specifically. A Black Management Development task force was set up at head office, consisting of senior white managers and directors and one African manager. This task force was responsible for driving the new focus. Operating companies were, however, responsible for setting their own targets over a five-year period. The advances made during the 1985–1993 period (9.5 percent African management) were significantly better than the South African average figure of 2 percent African managers. They were not, however, in line with the projected Unilever targets (1993 – 11 percent; 1998 – 23 percent).

Within the Unilever group, operating companies made different progress. This was primarily due to varied target setting and the extent to which affirmative action was prioritised in each company. Companies where more challenging targets were set generally made better progress. However, there has always been central monitoring via annual presentations to national management on targets and progress.

THE TARGET-SETTING PROCESS

Targets are integral to the way in which Unilever conducts its business and they have been an important mechanism in driving and monitoring the Unilever affirmative action initiative. Its target-setting process is outlined below:
- All human resource activities at a company level are reveiwed, culminating in a company personnel plan for the forthcoming year.
- Personnel plans are discussed by individual company boards for approval.
- Personnel plans are then submitted to the national management/board for review.
- Plans are then agreed or adjusted by the national management/board.
- Company personnel plans are then collated into the Unilever human resource development and affirmative action plans for the coming year.
- These plans are submitted to the London office. It has never issued a specific directive, but Unilever (SA) did report to the EEC code in the 1980s.

CURRENT STATUS (1994)

On reviewing its progress in June 1994, the company reformulated its approach to ensure greater commitment, focus and creativity. According to a senior human resource manager within the head office, the current approach is not fundamentally different to what was conceptualised in 1985:

What we started in 1985 is very similar to what we are currently doing. We covered our backs too much in the period between 1985 and 1993 and we were not prepared to take the risks – we were overly cautious in the 1980s. During this period we overlooked some of the problems identified in 1985. An important issue of relevance in 1985, and still relevant today, is that of rewarding people for being good developers. Unilever managers are among the most target- and task-oriented people you can find. It is built into our culture and reward system. We reward results. We are now beginning to tackle some of the issues that we knew about, but overlooked, in the 1980s. We are more focused now, but still need to standardise our affirmative action objectives across our operating companies as there has been differential progress across these companies to date.

FOCUS

Current affirmative action initiatives are focused on the development of African managers. In the debate on the way forward, it was felt that if affirmative action became all embracing it would lose focus. A further consideration was that significant achievements had been made at the work-force level, and that these were generally ahead of what other companies had achieved, or what the government or trade unions would expect. The trade unions have not, therefore, been consulted in the management affirmative action policy development process. Furthermore, according to a senior Unilever manager, African managers did not appear to see the unions as having a direct role in African management development.

ACCOUNTABILITY

In reviewing the 1985–1993 period, Unilever realised that target setting without real accountability was inadequate. The most important shift in its approach has been a greater appreciation of the importance of accountability. Although stated as a key business objective, affirmative action has never really been an enforceable component of performance management for Unilever managers. Bonuses for senior managers were based on overall company performance, but excluded affirmative action accomplishments.

Unilever management believes personnel have a (support) role, but it is now accepted that it needs to be firmly driven by commitment from the boardroom and translated into line management accountability. In support of this realisation an affirmative action task force was established to assist with policy communication and implementation. It consists of three African senior managers and four white senior managers. The terms of reference of the task force had to still be finalised by the time this research was completed, but is likely to include:

- Providing support for both companies and individuals during implementation.

- Facilitating organisational learning.
- Developing and implementing a two-way communication and feedback network.
- Implementing a monitoring system for measuring progress against long-term objectives.

Unilever's affirmative action effort has focused on the development of managerial potential and, since 1985, specifically on the development of African managers. It is important, therefore, to briefly outline its approach to management development. This is followed by a discussion of individual experiences and perceptions of affirmative action as ptactised within the company.

MANAGEMENT DEVELOPMENT AND AFFIRMATIVE ACTION

UNILEVER MANAGEMENT DEVELOPMENT

Unilever takes on 5–10 percent of its total management numbers in graduate (management) trainees each year. Since the early 1990s Unilever has aimed to increase the African graduate intake to 50 percent. Although its approach to management development has evolved over the years, the following guiding principles remain:

- Recruiting at least 5 percent of management strength annually as management trainees to ensure a regular supply of potential management talent. Trainees are drawn from South African universities during the annual "milk round" conducted by Unilever managers. Shortlisted candidates are then reviewed in panel interviews conducted by senior management.
- Recruiting and developing a quota of trainees, irrespective of the economic climate, since this is a long-term investment.
- Trainees joining the company are assessed to be "high potential" individuals.
- Trainees are given real jobs and responsibility with specific performance targets, beginning in their first year.
- Trainees and managers are exposed to structured functional and general management training to complement practical experience, and to ensure the building of more generalist skills. This is further encouraged by cross functional moves and secondments at management levels.
- Use is made of "high potential development lists". These development lists inform the annual business and personnel planning exercise for the coming year, and the next four years. Potential listings are used to focus the development of high potential people. Africans at senior staff and management levels may appear on both development and affirmative action listings. The latter specifically tracks and shapes the careers of high potential African managers.

The annual intake of graduate trainees is more than Unilever can digest, but this approach assures the company of a pool of management talent despite losses. Unilever world-wide has a reputation for its standard of management development, and has been cited as the business training university of the countries in which it operates. Traditionally, graduates have specifically targeted Unilever companies as a training and development ground.

RETENTION OF MANAGERS AND MANAGEMENT TRAINEES (1988 – 1993)

A critical issue for Unilever, and for all companies embarking on affirmative action initiatives, is understanding the reasons for the high turnover of African managers and trainees. Sixty-six percent of the African exits from 1991 to 1993 were due to improved prospects in other companies, in most cases to management jobs, and for improved working conditions. Only a third of the white graduate intake left in the same period, of which the vast majority went overseas to see what was happening in the outside world, rather than for better job prospects. During the past four years, Unilever (SA) has lost about 40 African managers.

Retention rates for white trainees and managers are considered by Unilever to be satisfactory. However, managers and trainees interviewed believed that Unilever was losing more (good) people than in the past. The reasons for Africans leaving are captured by the following responses:

> Many (white) managers in this company believe that Africans won't make it. Africans leave because they are frustrated and have no ownership of their jobs, and no clarity regarding what they need to do to qualify for promotion. (Interview with African manager.)

> Our white managers are misinterpreting the reasons why Africans leave. They believe that people leave for fantastic salaries. In some cases this is true. For the vast majority, Africans feel that Unilever provides excellent training, but does not provide sufficient opportunity for them to apply what they have learned. (Interview with senior white manager.)

Given the increasing trend towards the committed implementation of affirmative action in South Africa, a fluid market for educated and trained Africans is emerging. This is exacerbated by many South African companies paying unreasonable premiums for Africans rather than investing in the development process themselves. This creates a significant pull factor, but does not appear to be the root cause of the problem. African people interviewed said people left the company because of the continued polarisation in understanding, the poor perceptions of African ability, the lack of internal discussion and debate and alienation from the company culture. None of the

Africans interviewed said they would leave simply for a better package. Apart from those people with less than one year's working experience, all had been offered better financial packages from other companies or recruitment agencies. The following comments sum up these sentiments:

> Over and above race issues in particular, there are a host of people within the company that have not come to terms with the fact that the socio-political situation is undergoing fundamental change. There is a need to change the way people view Africans, African consumer behaviour, and Africans' ability to handle the business world. In dealing with Africans there is a preconceived notion that they come from a disadvantaged background, and that they (will) battle. The result is that when people want information or help they tend to bypass the African person and go directly to a "reliable source". (Interview with African marketing assistant.)

> If someone offered me much more than I am getting now, I would question why. I have friends who have moved to higher paying companies, but they eventually leave because they are not given anything to do. They sit and read the newspapers all day – and get paid for this! In some companies Africans are frustrated intentionally. In a country like South Africa, where we have been told repeatedly that Africans are not the same (as whites), some people genuinely believe that black people are inferior. They can't bring themselves to believe otherwise. (Interview with African assistant manager.)

PERCEPTIONS OF ORGANISATIONAL CULTURE

A related issue here is that of organisational culture and work environment. Table 4 overleaf shows the different perceptions of the Unilever culture. The core reading of the Unilever culture across these three categories appears consistent, with the African responses indicating concerns regarding alienation, support and feedback. The question is to what extent these issues contribute towards decisions to leave the company. The comments that follow indicate that the culture is changing, but it is still perceived to be an obstacle:

> Given that there are now more Africans attending universities, more young African graduates are entering South African organisations. African and white students perform in similar ways at university, but the African student finds it more difficult adjusting to the corporate or business culture. Unilever and individuals have a joint responsibility in this regard. If it does not work both parties ends up the loser. Africans are in the minority and it is taken for granted, given the similar experiences at university, that they will and must fit into the culture. The reality is that we all have to respect each other and make the effort to understand each other's culture. There are more people showing a real interest in understanding me, where I come from and my aspirations. There is willingness to compromise. (Interview with African management trainee.)

The culture is based on white English culture. There are Afrikaans guys who are just as frustrated here. Whites know more about what is expected from them, mostly because of their social life and their discussions of the business and the information they get up front. The most important thing is that you get sidelined because you don't know what you need to do to get promoted. White guys are pushy and seen as assertive, but if the African guy is pushy he is seen as arrogant. They expect you to do the same things, but when you do they have different ways of looking at it – and think of you as a "cheeky kaffir". (Interview with African manager.)

A further consideration here is how providing preferential opportunities for African managers and trainees has an affect on the morale and commitment of white managers and trainees. Although there was acceptance of the need to provide such opportunities, white managers and trainees expressed concerns about standards and the future of their own careers. White women were particularly concerned about the latter issue:

Many of our (African) graduates get a job offer once a week and the dilemma is, do I sit here and wait for the experience or take a chance in the marketplace? I am ready for promotion, but I know the next person to be promoted will be black. These are issues we are all finding difficult to deal with. (Interview with assistant manager.)

■ TABLE 4 ■

PERCEPTIONS OF UNILEVER CULTURE — KEY WORDS FROM INTERVIEWS

WHITE MEN:	International; Demanding; Stable; Stressful; Hard Work; Political; Professional; Paternal; A Focus on Achievement; Caring and a Regard for Colleagues; In a State of Flux; Moving from Top Down to Participation; Task Focus; Lack of People Orientation.
BLACK MEN & WOMEN:	Conservative; Profit oriented; Eurocentric; Impersonal; Arrogant; White; Middle Class; Big; Political; Results at all Costs; Ruthless Grapevine; Unilateral Decision Making; Step-On-One-Another; Excellent Training; Rewarding and Stimulating; Professional; Pressured; Unforgiving; Informal; Customer Oriented; Limited Feedback for Blacks; Competitive; Withholding of Information; Ignores Individual Feelings.
WHITE WOMEN:	Competitive; Good Training; Demanding; Pressured; Hard Work; High Expectations; Professional; Positive.

Senior managers in Unilever are aware of the issues outlined above, and are particularly concerned about African perceptions of the internal environment. The recent reformulation of affirmative action policy and the new task group are beginning to address the issues of culture, development opportunities, retention and white career anxieties.

AFRICAN LOBBY GROUPS AND CONSULTATION

Affirmative action has historically been driven and owned by white management, and there has been little attempt to involve and consult African managers. Of all the people interviewed, it was only the more senior white managers who could clearly articulate the company's position on affirmative action. Even at this level, each person provided a different version of policy, targets and progress to date. It was only after the reformulation of the affirmative action strategy, and the development of a formal written policy in 1994, that a coherent communication exercise was implemented.

Given this low level of consultation and communication, a number of African lobby groups emerged in the 1980s. These took the form of support groups for African managers at the various operating sites. Although they raised an awareness of concerns, they did not develop sufficient stature to make real impact. More recently, however, African managers in the Black Managers' Initiative presented a position paper to senior Unilever managers and board members. This initiative led to the emergence of a new spirit of consultation on affirmative action. It has also strengthened African involvement in the drafting of the Unilever affirmative action policy.

This shift towards consultation and joint problem solving is also happening at company, functional and departmental levels. For example, a number of presentations have been made by African managers to the Lever Brothers directors and senior management. A synopsis of the issues that have been raised in these forums follows:

- Recruitment, assessment and selection policies and practices.
- The implementation of international practices, without due consideration for the uniqueness of the South African context.
- Inappropriate prescribed qualities and skills criteria for assessing management potential.
- A lack of due consideration of individuals' cultural backgrounds.
- Biased perceptions of Africans' ability.
- Insufficient use of African recruiters on selection panels.
- Retention of African managers and trainees.
- A lack of support from line management.
- Line management is not held accountable for the development of people, or for the development of Africans in particular.
- Affirmative action strategies are sound, but are not properly implemented or clearly communicated throughout the organisation.
- The need to realise that even non-high flyers should be developed.

- African expectations are sometimes unrealistic.
- Training. The training offered was considered to be excellent.

Although these discussions and debates represent a significant move forward, such interactions have taken place between senior white managers and African managers only. They have not included white middle management, African trainees or white trainees. This approach does not take into consideration white anxieties or concerns. A white trainee said:

> Communication regarding affirmative action is poor and our department has not achieved much to date. The (white) management called all the Africans in our department together to discuss affirmative action, and why it was not working. We were opposed to this and asked why we were not included. We still do not know what is going on, and this concerns me.

LEVER BROTHERS MARKETING DEPARTMENT

Developments in the Lever Brothers marketing department represent a deeper level of consultation and joint problem solving. The entire department, from graduate trainee to director level, has become involved in working groups commissioned to solve a range of work related problems, including more creative approaches to the successful implementation of affirmative action. The triggers for this have been a number of simultaneous crises outlined below. The solutions adopted represent a merger of improved departmental effectiveness, good people management and workable affirmative action.

THE THREE 'CRISES'

BUSINESS INNOVATION AND WORK CULTURE

Lever Brothers, in line with the Unilever global detergents strategy, has been undergoing compound innovation and change in order to ensure future competitiveness. New technology, systems and work processes – coupled with multiple product launches – have collectively placed tremendous pressure on the marketing department over the past two years. In addition, the culture of this department is characterised as highly individualistic, competitive, task- rather than people-oriented and unforgiving.

RELATIVELY INEXPERIENCED JUNIOR TO MIDDLE MANAGEMENT

Given the loss of key managers during the past two years, the department was left with relatively inexperienced brand managers and stretched marketing managers. Marketing managers were on a learning curve of their own, resulting in a task, rather than a people, focus and were particularly inexperienced at managing new recruits.

■ TABLE 5 ■

MARKETING DEPARTMENT STRUCTURE

LEVEL	WHITE MEN	WHITE WOMEN	BLACK MEN	BLACK WOMEN	TOTAL	MEN	WOMEN
MANAGER	6	10	1	0	17	7	10
ASSIST MANAGER	1	3	0	1	5	1	4
MARKETING ASSISTANT	2	5	1	4	12	3	9
TOTAL	9	18	2	5	34	11	23
	(26%)	(53%)	(6%)	(15%)	(100%)	(32%)	(68%)

AFFIRMATIVE ACTION

The commitment to affirmative action has resulted in a number of African marketing assistant appointments in an environment that does not provide the necessary support.

THE CONSULTATION AND PROBLEM-SOLVING PROCESS

The first two crises had been brewing for some time and were viewed by some to be creating high levels of stress and general dissatisfaction. One person believed the work environment to be the key contributor to people leaving the department. Although not necessarily directly related, the under performance of a new marketing assistant, and the mismanagement of this under performance, brought these three crises to a head. The incident below provides a synopsis of the unfolding of events:

SYNOPSIS – ASSISTANT CASE

A new assistant was recruited who, in retrospect, was not a suitable candidate for a position in a particular department.

According to the other department assistants interviewed, the company did not provide a sufficiently realistic insight into what the assistant job entailed. It also did not explain what one was expected to achieve and the pressure one would be expected to work under. The induction provided was also seen to be inadequate. African managers and management trainees were also critical of performance management, support and the "distant" involvement of the personnel department.

Given the pressured work environment and the focus on tasks rather than people, the person involved did not ask for and/or was not provided with the necessary support. Her first manager was not considered to have particularly good people management skills. English was not her first language, and good written and verbal skills were required to perform adequately in this job.

It became clear after six months that this person was really battling. The "grapevine opinion" had by then taken root and her chances of survival in the department or anywhere else in the organisation was minimal. Nobody wanted to inherit a "failure". The "unwritten rule" was that the person should read the writing on the wall and leave before it really got out of hand.

The person's self confidence started to crumble and the other African trainees formed a "black caucus" to provide support. Management discussed the issue among themselves, and the two "groupings" became more and more "suspicious" of one another. Perceptions became more and more polarised, but there was still no open discussion or attempt to solve the problem jointly.

Meanwhile nine months had passed, by which time the person had had three different managers, none of whom really wanted to inherit this "problem".

The situation became untenable and the person left the company. This account was constructed from different narratives, and weaves through the divergent versions offered. The immediate outcome was emotional tension and racial polarisation. The resolution and learning process started with the department director calling a forum to discuss the future of graduate development in the department. This subsequently developed into three interesting projects aimed at improving work efficiency, developing better people management skills and improving graduate (management) development. In each project team the guiding principle was joint problem solving, achieved by including people at all levels in the department. Project teams conduct their own investigations leading to proposals to the department for discussion, after which the agreed components are implemented. A brief outline of these ongoing projects follows.

WORK SMARTER NOT HARDER

This project is co-ordinated by the marketing assistants and is aimed at better management of the day-to-day working environment, specifically operational, procedural and process activities. After a general discussion with all marketing assistants and assistant brand managers, the project group split up into teams to investigate and then submit proposals for the following:

- Time consuming administration – the use of administrative support staff for photocopying; collecting and delivering parcels; buying competitors' products, setting up meeting rooms; preparing budgets and processing invoices; the use of secretaries and the allocation of telephones.
- Communication (inter/intra departmental).
- Presentations – briefing, standardisation and the purchase of upgraded equipment.

- Graduate Induction – a three-week induction format; and a longer programme running concurrently with on-the-job training.

In future this will become a standard project for new marketing assistants each year. "Work smarter" will be a feature of the work-related introduction to the business and will be supplemented by a more structured introduction to the corporate and departmental culture.

PEOPLE MANAGEMENT SKILLS

This project is aimed at reviewing the approach to people management and implementing a more objective performance assessment process. The introduction of 360 degree appraisals (upward, peer and internal client ratings of individual performance) has been introduced. More weighting will in future be given to a manager's performance in the area of developing people. In addition, more frequent informal assessment has been recommended. It has also been agreed that marketing managers will coach, develop and actively share their management experience with (new) brand managers.

GRADUATE DEVELOPMENT

The two previous projects lead into, and inform, this project. The purpose is to improve the entry and early development experiences for new management trainees. Marketing assistants, assistant brand managers and brand managers have made independent recommendations, some of which are listed below:
- Realistic briefings to potential candidates at the university recruitment stage – realistic job previews.
- A review of the current selection criteria, with a greater focus on actual job requirements.
- Job specific induction and more involvement by marketing management in the induction process.
- A review of entry level training, with an emphasis on the involvement of different levels of management as appropriate.
- The realisation that the work culture is alienating for some people, and that this impacts directly on performance and tenure.
- Standardised assessment of progress. A standardised set of tasks and objectives for marketing assistants to achieve within set periods during their first six to 12 months has been constructed. A progress matrix indicating the different levels of achievement expected across core tasks and specific time periods has been proposed and will be piloted and refined. The progress matrix is: first progress report after three months; the first performance appraisal after eight months; the second performance appraisal after one year and the third performance appraisal after 16 months.
- Corresponding to the above time periods, each core task or objective will be

assessed at increasingly complex levels, as indicated below:

Level 1: Needs working knowledge of activities and operations.

Level 2: Takes responsibility for basic systems with little supervision. Needs working knowledge of company systems.

Level 3: Takes complete responsibility with limited supervision. Contributes to complex systems as agreed. Makes recommendations for improvement. Can run a project meeting if required.

Level 4: Leads Project. Works independently. Takes ownership.

The three ongoing projects outlined above are contributing to both work process improvements and the development of a more open work environment and culture. This has been made possible through a process of consultation and involvement. The key lessons emerging from this process are as follows:

- "Crises" are often the triggers for change.
- Consultation and joint problem solving leads to more committed and integrated solutions.
- "Crisis" situations can be avoided if a more open culture is established – a culture that encourages consultation and inclusion, and one that is open to questioning its own assumptions.
- There is a need for greater balance between tasks and people.
- Successful affirmative action strategies require good management practice, rather than "treating people differently".
- A change of culture, and the successful implementation of affirmative action, requires the accountable commitment of senior management.
- Change can, therefore, occur in "pockets" rather than at an organisational level.

CONCLUSION

Unilever has made a significant contribution to management development in South Africa and has, during the past 20 years, made considerable progress against its own rolling affirmative action targets. In today's terms, its early approach to affirmative action may appear conservative, but in the 1970s it was considered to be pioneering. By 1985, senior management clearly understood what was required for the successful implementation of affirmative action.

However, this was not openly communicated throughout the organisation, which resulted in varied commitment across the operating companies. A related issue was that of loosely defined accountability and the lack of recognition for achievements. Until very recently the process was driven and owned by white management, with little attempt to actively engage in a process of consultation and involvement. The trade unions are still not considered a key stakeholder in the process of developing African managers.

The focus on developing African managers is important in that it helps redefine power relations and legitimacy in the organisation. The development of African managers only is, however, not a sufficient response and a more integrated approach could yield greater benefits in the long term.

A distinct feature of the implementation of black advancement in the 1980s, and affirmative action in the 1990s, has been the inability of South African organisations to learn from one another's mistakes and successes. In conclusion, therefore, the key insights from the Unilever case study are summarised below:

- The affirmative action policy needs to be clearly and consistently articulated across all levels in the company.
- Targets and timetables are essential and should be standardised across all operating companies.
- The successful implementation of affirmative action requires clear accountability, related directly to the performance assessment of all managers and to the bonuses of senior management.
- Unilateral decision making and ownership by white managers is limiting, and real solutions lie in consultation and joint problem solving at group, company, departmental and individual levels.
- Given the greater availability of qualified and educated African people, the retention of good people has become the most critical component of any affirmative action initiative. This requires a review of the entire staffing and development process.
- Company culture and the negative perceptions of African ability are powerful inhibiting factors in the development of African managers and trainees. They are the principle reason for the high turnover of African people.
- The lack of senior role models and the high turnover of African people suggests to new recruits that the company offers a training ground rather than a long-term career. This prevents the achievement of the necessary critical mass of African managers that ensures that affirmative action develops its own momentum.
- Although significant progress has been made in the development of women and their promotion to management positions, there are no women at board level. Women do not constitute a key affirmative action target group. White women are particularly concerned about the impact of affirmative action on their careers.
- In general, insufficient attention is paid to white anxieties about affirmative action.
- Affirmative action is seen as the development of African managers, rather than the development of Africans and women across organisational levels. ■

THE SOWETAN

PELIWE LOLWANA

PROFILE OF THE COMPANY

The Sowetan newspaper was previously known as the World. Most staff who
have been with the company since those days still remember how the walls
needed to be painted, there were no pictures in the offices and threadbare
carpets contributed to the depressing atmosphere in the building. The general
manager at the time the research was conducted, who is white, still remembers
his disgust at the terrible conditions when he first joined the paper at the
beginning of 1989. When he commented on this, he was told it was futile to
improve conditions as "blacks will take the carpets and pictures away from the
walls anyway".

That was the beginning of a long road travelled by the former general
manager and the company to prove that this assertion was wrong. It was a hard
task, but made possible by the fact that his co-manager, the chief editor, who is
black, shared his unswerving commitment to the paper and what it stood for.

In theory, both managers held equivalent powers in the company. In
practice, the general manager carried greater day-to-day responsibility for the
running of the company. This was partly to do with the general manager's
personal qualities as a forceful, highly organised and disciplined person. The
arrangement also freed the chief editor to do what he does best, as a public
figure and a creator of ideas that help develop public support for the Sowetan.

The chemistry between these two managers contributed significantly to the
transformation of the Sowetan from the dreary conditions of the past to the
highly energetic, friendly, casual and freshly decorated environment of today.
The changes are not only confined to environmental appearances. The staff
complement has also changed to reflect the black majority who are the major
readers of the Sowetan.

The mission of the Sowetan has developed over the years and the paper is
now generally known as a black voice and a black story for a black audience.
All agree that the business success of the paper can be attributed to the fact

that consumers identify with the paper. The chief editor is not only a well-placed member of the community but has also managed to put the Sowetan at the centre of the national agenda through, for example, the popular Nation Building Programme, a campaign conducted throughout its pages to engage readers in a programme of black empowerment.

During the hard years that have seen other newspapers go under, the fortunes of the Sowetan have turned around from a loss of about R500 000 a year to a profit of about R12 million a year. The newspaper now reaches 1,6 million readers daily. They are predominantly young, black, urban residents of Gauteng, the most densely populated region of South Africa. Demographics show that this is the fastest growing area of South Africa and the Sowetan therefore has the potential to reach even more people in the future.

Recently the Sowetan was bought from the Argus conglomerate by New Africa Investments Ltd. A 1993 Media and Marketing Research (MMR) survey showed that 22 percent of those interviewed thought that this kind of unbundling was a good idea, as opposed to only 9 percent who felt anxious about the move. These statistics do not reflect the major impact that the unbundling has had on staff. The issue was mentioned frequently during interviews and will be raised again under a separate heading.

METHOD AND SAMPLE

The case study of the Sowetan was conducted in March/April 1994. The interviewee sample by job level was as follows:

■ TABLE 1 ■		
	EDITORIAL	MANAGEMENT
SENIOR MANAGERS	1	1
MANAGERS/EDITORS	1	3
MIDDLE MANAGEMENT	2	3
STAFF	1	3

HISTORY OF AFFIRMATIVE ACTION

BLACK AND GENDER ADVANCEMENT

The first opportunity for black advancement at the Sowetan emerged between 1990 and 1991, when the Argus set aside funds to be spent over a three-year period for black advancement in all its subsidiaries. The Sowetan took greater advantage of this programme than any of the other Argus companies. The company spent the bulk of this money on training its staff in a broad range of skills that were not always directly job-related. A category of additional posts was also created so that qualified people could be brought into the company, even though suitable positions were not immediately available. At the time, the fact that the Argus had made available resources to do this was helpful, but the Sowetan would probably have found resources to do this anyway. The whole process was driven by a strong commitment to transforming the company to reflect its readers. It is therefore not surprising that after three years the composition of the staff has changed completely.

■ TABLE 2 ■

1994 STAFF PROFILE

WHITE MALE	8%
WHITE FEMALE	14%
ASIAN MALE	2%
ASIAN FEMALE	3%
COLOURED MALE	2%
COLOURED FEMALE	6%
AFRICAN MALE	50%
AFRICAN FEMALE	15%
TOTAL	100%

The Sowetan has also put enormous effort into changing the racial composition of its management. In 1990, there were no black managers. By 1994, nine out of 12 managers were black.

Gender advancement seems to be one of the weaker areas in the company's transformation. Even though women are not totally excluded from circles of power, they are still weakly represented in management structures. The current management ratio is 3.5:1 in favour of men.

The changes in the Sowetan seem to have been personally driven by the general manager rather than the result of a stated or clear and explicit company policy. As he said:

> I make all the appointments. If I do not make them myself, I approve them – all
> senior appointments – and I need black people. So I only employ people who
> are not white. I would not be obsessive about that if I thought there was a very
> significant reason for employing a white person. On balance, my argument is
> that this is a fundamentally black organisation serving a black community and

should be manned by black people. If I was transported to Sydney, Australia as
the general manager, I probably would not do as good a job as an Australian
manager working in the Australian market. And I think this is the rational and
sensible reason for us to have black managers at the Sowetan.

The general manager has subsequently been promoted, but the commitment
from his office created an environment that facilitated change easily in the
company. One could argue that it could have taken much longer if, for
example, the impetus for transforming the company had come only from the
bottom. However, some employees still had reservations about the extent to
which real power had shifted in the company. This perception was fuelled by
an incident that was uppermost in people's minds at the time of this study.

Two highly qualified black business school graduates had been appointed
with the aim of grooming them so that one of them would eventually take over
the general management of the company. But both graduates resigned, within
six weeks of each other, after only one year at the company.

This left the staff confused and with conflicting perspectives about what
had really happened. Some staff blamed management for not having made
room for, and provided support for, them. Others thought the resignations were
to be expected as black managers were a scarce commodity and poachers are
ever ready for a slightly dissatisfied black manager. Others thought that the
two new employees were just too greedy, expected too much and could not
resist better offers. Many staff members simply thought that the pressure for
the final prize – to replace the general manager – was too great and something
had to give.

The case of the two black managers might be insignificant when compared
to the many successes that the Sowetan has had. However, there are lessons
that should be learned. No matter what the truth was, the fact is that two black
business managers did not work out at an organisation that is committed to
being owned, managed and staffed by black people. Although initially some
perceived the issue as a white management versus black employee issue, the
truth is not that simple. It is important to note that the staff's reactions to this
incident were not racially divided with blacks reacting in a particular way and
whites in another. There seems to have been a general consensus that the
Sowetan could have done more to integrate these two into the company. It was
acknowledged by most interviewees that there were natural cliques that often
transcended racial groupings. They revolved around teamwork and formed
support groups for most people in the organisation. The new recruits, who had
not worked their way through the organisation, were naturally not part of these
networks.

The difficult position of the new recruits was further exacerbated by the
fact that, as managers, they were in an awkward position vis-a-vis unions and
other managers. One belonged to the union, although he did not seem to have
been very active. The other did not belong to the union.

While they constantly had to prove to their seniors that they were strong, competent and could deliver no matter what, they had the decks stacked against them. They could not appeal to management as that would have exposed their vulnerability and they were not quite part of the workers and, therefore, could not make full use of union support. They were therefore in a no-win situation.

As contenders for the same job, the two newcomers were not even able to rely on each other as they were in competition with each other. Above all, they were recruited on the basis of their academic qualifications and work experience elsewhere, and did not stay long enough to imbibe some of the Sowetan culture and ethos. Being outsiders must have worked against them so strongly that, no matter how good they were, it would have been difficult to survive.

This experience speaks volumes about the limitations of external recruitment. Outside candidates may need greater induction, training and support than internal candidates, irrespective of their academic qualifications and experiences. There is also something to be said about the appropriateness (or lack) of individuals with general training in business management. Both external appointments and generalised qualifications may not provide an easy route to the implementation of affirmative action.

There is another side to the story that is seldom talked about. This concerns the pain and the hurt of staff, management and new recruits that comes with failures in the transformation process. Recalling the dark days when the resignation of the two managers was a very emotive issue – and some white managers blamed themselves or were blamed – one white manager said:

> After the issue of ... these guys leaving ... I was very unhappy. I was desperately emotional about it. I cried a lot ... I felt it was unfair on him (former general manager) ... I looked at the things he has done and changed here. So how could they say that white management does not care for black managers? They must look at the facts. I felt it was grossly unfair that they could condemn him when he had given the biggest opportunity to people than anyone else in the Argus company, never mind the Sowetan – and he could be attacked like that?

The former general manager remembered the pain and the hurt he experienced while going through the experience by saying that "in management courses they never talk about the pain and anguish of management".

TRANSFORMING THE CULTURE AND ETHOS

The issue of empowerment at the Sowetan is many-layered. As a newspaper the Sowetan will not tolerate being silenced. As a black newspaper, the Sowetan has produced a work-force that is steeped in protest politics. Management has created an environment where very open communication is encouraged. There are weekly meetings where all staff members are involved in the running of the company. Staff attitude surveys[1] show that the Sowetan was the best communicator with its staff in the Argus group.

Right from the beginning, when non-racialism was not fashionable, the Sowetan made a point of discussing racism. The former general manager also openly declared war on anyone who was a racist. The company has put a lot of resources into developing and training staff and management is appraised by workers. As one would expect, these steps have created an enabling environment for staff development, especially for those from disadvantaged communities.

Two years ago, the Sowetan staff began a process of discovering each other's cultures. The period was characterised by some bad luck, tensions in the company and generally very low morale. Someone mentioned that in black communities this would call for a "cleansing" ceremony to get rid of the bad spirits. To the amazement of most, this suggestion was met with enthusiasm by the former general manager. Later, he said: "If this is an experience of the majority of people in this country every weekend, let us do it."

The cleansing ceremony has become an annual event and includes the slaughtering of goats on company grounds and the drinking of traditional beer. The purpose of the ceremony is to appease the ancestors so that they, in return, can mediate with the Creator. When staff were asked what they thought of the ritual, there were some animated responses. Some think it is the most unifying experience they've ever had. Some think it is a good opportunity to party. Some think it ridicules black culture. Some – including some blacks – think it is "unChristian" and some think it is "cute and exotic". This is certainly a custom that distinguishes the Sowetan from many other companies. There is already talk about bringing in some of other groups' cultural activities into the company. For example, the Muslims planned to share their festive activities for the end-of-fast period.

The ceremony contributed greatly to creating a space for those who have historically been marginalised in the culture of South African companies. For the first time, others take a back seat and let the disadvantaged people tell them how to do things – they have something to share which they feel is appreciated by others. The traditionalists, who tend to occupy the lower levels in the employment structures, are custodians of knowledge on this custom and therefore qualify for a special place in conducting the ceremony. In itself this has a tremendous impact on their sense of empowerment.

On another level, the ceremony calls for the examination of the participants' spirituality, beliefs and their subconscious and conscious thoughts about religion. The ceremony evoked a number of questions for the researcher: What has happened over the centuries to this cultural practice the Sowetan is bringing to the work-place? What does it do to the wounds that have been gaping over the centuries? Is it right to bring what is considered to

---

1. *This refers to the* Sowetan Staff Attitude Survey Report *of May 1993, prepared by Marketing and Media Research for the Sowetan.*

be a private family practice to a public place like work? Will there be a time when the ceremony is not necessary at the Sowetan? It is, however, essential to acknowledge that this is a uniquely South African and creative way of dealing with problems at work and deserves commendation.

Language has also been a significant contributing factor to the maintenance and advancement of a specific culture in South African companies. English is the language of business at the Sowetan, but some people sometimes use their home languages and thereby exclude those who do not speak these languages. When this happens it tends to create impenetrable walls, and makes it difficult for language to assist in establishing a homogeneous culture. Language was often seen as the basis on which English first language speakers discriminated against, and judged, others. One person said that, on the whole, white employees did not seem to have patience with those who did not speak English as a first language. As the language debates continue on the national platform, it can be expected that further real conflicts over the use of language will be felt on company floors.

TRANSFORMATION THROUGH PARTICIPATIVE MANAGEMENT

Participative management is one of the transformation approaches introduced at the Sowetan. According to management, it has brought positive changes in the communication ethos in the company. There are weekly meetings where nothing is sacred and staff can question any aspect of the company. No matter who I talked to, there was no shuffling and avoiding issues – employees exuded confidence. They did not have to agree with management or unions or any other interest group. As an observer in the meetings, I could clearly see that participation levels were high for all staff and there were few barriers that inhibited communication. Most staff interviewed regarded participation positively as they felt it was a good way to redistribute management power and enable all employees to be involved in the decision-making process. As the next step in participative management, staff were offered shares in the new holding company of the Sowetan.

While management had opened up avenues for communication and participation, some staff were still concerned about the effectiveness of the policy. The Media Workers Association of South Africa (an affiliate of the National Council of Trade Unions) was critical of the extent to which participation was entrenched in the organisation. Although the union admitted that at least a process had begun that included all staff, it was quick to point out that:

> Management still has the monopoly on decision-making and will not consult
> with the union on such crucial issues such as the "unbundling" of the paper,
> and even on strategic planning for the company ... management is under the
> illusion that everyone feels included as long as there are frequent meetings.

However, it was evident that the union was just beginning to grapple with the issue of affirmative action in the company. The implication was that the union had not been a major force in the implementation of affirmative action and could not take credit for the changes that had taken place.

EFFECTS OF EXTERNAL POWER SHIFTS

On the surface, the future of the Sowetan seems guaranteed. There is a sense of ownership among those who work there and the staff complement is close to reflecting the demographics of the country, yet there is still a sense of unease. The most important reason for this seems to be the recent unbundling of the Sowetan to New Africa Investments Ltd.

Previously employees at the Sowetan fought against a company that was white and male-dominated and this gave them a rallying point against a common enemy, namely the Argus group. However, this enemy had a long record of economic success and therefore the Sowetan staff did not feel insecure about their future.

The perceived alignment of the new owners with the ANC also seems to have struck a raw nerve with staff members. A 1993 MMR survey showed that of the 57 percent of staff that answered the question, only 18 percent would have voted for the ANC.

Both economic viability and independence seemed to be the uppermost concerns in the minds of the Sowetan staff as their future is entrusted to "untested" owners who seemed to have strong ties to a political party. In general, the Sowetan staff were shocked by the lack of communication about the deal and about how suddenly it took place. The sale has the potential to disturb the internal processes that have carefully been put in place and leave staff with a sense of disempowerment. The unbundling at the Sowetan is just one example of the changing order that we might expect in the future. Employees have to be prepared and nurtured through this process.

EVALUATION OF THE POLICY

The Sowetan's experience makes one realise that there is not one recipe for affirmative action that can be implemented by all. However, there are general trends that are relevant to most companies.

It is evident that the Sowetan has come a long way in transforming its racial composition and culture. It may seem strange that in this "black" company the driving force of change was a white general manager. This dispels one of the myths of affirmative action. The general manager played a critical role in mediating between the white, conservative Argus group and the active, vocal staff at the Sowetan who demanded change. He also took personal responsibility for the risks associated with untested appointments and for nurturing new recruits. As the champion of the policies, he also took the brunt of the expressed anger, anguish and pain.

However, one begins to wonder what will happen now that the general manager has moved on. Will he be replaced by someone with a similar drive and commitment to transformation? The problem is that the intention to transfer ultimate management powers to black hands is blocked by the lack of available and trained candidates. Without systematic planning integrally linked to the affirmative action process, many companies might find themselves in a similar position of not having appropriate people to fill key positions. Once the new recruits are appointed, their proper induction and integration is crucial for affirmative action to succeed.

A further issue of concern is that the affirmative action policy at the Sowetan has not been supported by clear evaluation policies. It is difficult to see how progress and performance will be objectively monitored and assessed without clear, articulated performance criteria. The issue of competence is an example, which was often raised in interviews, especially with reference to the two black managers who had left. Some employees felt that they were not competent enough and therefore could not cope. However, they had no yardstick or feedback on which to base this judgement. Others felt that it was possible to measure competence by looking at who was inside and outside the senior management's clique.

The assessment of competence tends to be subjective and may be clouded by personal inclinations. The establishment of clear, objective criteria helps to remove the cloud of vagueness and improves the transparency of human resource practices.

Another important lesson from the Sowetan is the different aspects of a supporting environment for affirmative action. Strong direction from the chief editor was critical for success. The importance of creating a cultural space for workers was also acknowledged. The cleansing ceremony may not be replicated in other companies, but it is important that companies find other ways of creating this space.

A lesson can also be learned from the unsettling effect on staff of the change in ownership. We are living in a rapidly changing country. When the interviews were conducted early in 1994, the country did not yet enjoy a new government and constitution. These momentous events are still going to have ripple effects at an individual and organisational level. The unbundling at the Sowetan is just one example of the changing order that we might expect in the future. This experience underscores the importance of communicating about external changes with staff, especially when communication channels are already in place.

It is difficult to judge whether it was right for the Sowetan to have first concentrated on race before considering other target groups; or whether it should have included all disadvantaged groups from the beginning. The fact is that internal staffing programmes will need to shift focus to address the issue of women's participation in the company. The danger is that the initial enthusiasm and driving force may not be as strong as it was before. As long as there is no policy directly addressing gender participation, however, it will be difficult to plan for a totally inclusive organisation.

There are companies where staff profiles are clearly linked to strategic interests. The case of the Sowetan dispels the myth that affirmative action is antithetical to profitability. In fact, transforming the staff profile should be seen as a non-negotiable in a company with a consumer profile such as the Sowetan. Some organisations may not be faced with such a clear situation, but it is almost unimaginable that there are some that would not want to have a maximum impact on all communities in the country.

CONCLUSION

The Sowetan has reached a critical level of success in its transformation. Staff composition and leadership have changed substantially over the last four years. The cultural experiences of all employees have been broadened and an atmosphere of tolerance and inclusion is being actively created. There are already indications that this transformation has improved the paper's economic position over the past year and a half. But it has not been without cost. In the words of the former general manager, affirmative action should not be attempted by those who are not committed to it. It involves taking risks. It involves believing and trusting in others. Above all, it involves being conscious of the fact that failures are also personal and not just generalised. The pain of failure is felt by individuals, appointees, managers and all other staff. ■

ESKOM (ELECTRICITY SUPPLY COMMISSION)

SHELLEY VAN DER MERWE

PROFILE OF THE COMPANY

Eskom produces 98 percent of South Africa's electricity and employs nearly 40 000 people. It supplies more than half the total electricity consumed in Africa and, at the end of 1993, had total assets of R44,4 billion. It is currently the fifth largest utility company in the world. With these figures in mind, it is not surprising that Eskom is looked to for leadership by much of the business community in South Africa. This is not a common reputation for a former parastatal. Yet it is Eskom's history as a parastatal that makes it such an interesting case study for affirmative action.

Eskom does not have any shareholders as it is a public utility. It is funded entirely from debt and accumulated reserves. Under the Eskom Act of 1987 and the Electricity Act of 1987, the Electricity Council was established as the governing body of Eskom. This body is made up of representatives from government, industry, community-based consumers and, more recently, organised labour. The chairperson of the Electricity Council is a government appointee. The day-to-day running of Eskom is managed by the management board.

The changing customer base of Eskom, combined with trade union militancy and broader socio-political changes in South Africa, have significantly contributed to the reshaping of Eskom over the years. According to a senior corporate strategist, changes Eskom has made in restructuring, staffing and recruitment policies "cannot be viewed in isolation from the broader socio-political landscape. As an organisation, Eskom was shaped by the events taking place around it".

Eskom's consumer profile has changed substantially over the years, from initially supplying only industry to now supplying the domestic electricity market as well. Moreover, with the current political and economic changes under way, Eskom intends to expand its electricity delivery further into Africa.

As part of its restructuring, in 1992 (when the work-force was reduced from 66 000 to 40 000), Eskom management and trade unions agreed to "develop and institute processes to provide for the meaningful influence of trade unions over decisions that affect them as key stakeholders". Entitled "Eskom's Unfolding Vision", participatory structures were put in place at all levels of the organisation to provide regular forums to discuss pressing concerns and share information.

Eskom was the first organisation of its size in South Africa to undertake such an agreement with organised labour. The intention was admirable and has produced some success in some areas of Eskom. However, the culture of participation is taking time to filter down into the daily procedures and structures of the various components of Eskom's decentralised structure. Although these agreements were made at a time when Eskom was trying to promote an affirmative action policy, the restructuring and Unfolding Vision processes were not directly integrated with these aims.

As a technically oriented organisation, Eskom has, for many years, been sensitive to skills shortages in the country. How this need has been met has, as a result of it being a parastatal, been a highly politicised process. Eskom's first experience of affirmative action can be traced back to 1948, when Afrikaner men were targeted for senior positions, promotions, training and bursaries. It took about a generation for Afrikaners to move into the previously English-speaking dominated technical positions. But English-speaking managers still tend to retain many of the senior managerial positions.

More recently, the first concrete steps towards promoting a company-wide equal opportunity employment policy can be traced back to 1985, according to *Eskom News*, November 1985. A quantitative picture of Eskom's progress with affirmative action since 1985 cannot be presented as such records were not preserved. However, current staffing figures are as shown in the table overleaf.

Eskom's various functions and "groups" include generation, distribution, transmission, technology, services, finance, electrification, human resources, marketing and, more recently, growth and development. These are decentralised to such an extent that it is difficult to generalise about the organisation and its institutional culture in particular. One senior general manager said:

> You can't homogenise Eskom — which is part of why generalisations about
> affirmative action at Eskom are such a joke. (Interview, June 1994.)

The decentralised structure of Eskom tends to promote the development of local institutional cultures that are strongly shaped by dominant managerial styles and geographical locations. The manner in which policies are developed further emphasises the differentiated nature of Eskom's various functions and groups. The executive directors of each group develop directives with input from divisional human resource branches and line management. Only

■ TABLE 1 ■

PERMANENT STAFF STRENGTH BY RACE, GENDER AND SKILL LEVEL. MARCH 31, 1994.

PATERSON GRADE	WHITE	BLACK	COLOURED	ASIAN	TOTAL	WOMEN
F	17	5	0	0	22	1
E 4-5						
E 1-3	190	9	1	2	202	4
D 4-5	289	14	1	0	304	11
D 1-3	1 731	74	12	18	1 835	161
C 4-5	4 380	176	36	49	4 641	532
C 1-3	4 988	481	101	107	5 677	748
B	7 772	7 033	1 203	131	16 139	3391
A	0	10 359	932	1	11 298	187
TOTAL	19 367	18 151	2 286	308	40 118	5 035

Source: UCT Graduate School of Business — Breakwater Monitor

Notes:

Paterson F	Executive Directors
Paterson E 4-5	Senior — Executive Management
Paterson E 1-3	Senior Management
Paterson D 4-5	Middle — Senior Management
Paterson D 1-3	Junior — Middle Management
Paterson C 4-5	Assistant Management — Senior Supervisory & Junior Professional
Paterson C 1-3	Graduate Entry, Supervisory, Artisan & Technician, Senior Operative & Senior Admin/Clerical/Secretarial
Paterson B	Operative, Admin/Clerical/Secretarial
Paterson A	Entry Level Operative & Labourer

particularly contentious issues, such as affirmative action, are taken to the management board for discussion.

The decentralised structure of Eskom significantly contributes to, as one Eskom consultant put it, "a dynamic working atmosphere at the regional offices' level, with improved customer services that would be unlikely to exist with heavy central control". (Interview, July 1994.)

However, during the 53 interviews conducted, certain recurrent themes surfaced. Eskom's technical orientation is a strong feature in the various sectors of the organisation. As one manager put it: "If it isn't in numbers, it doesn't exist for Eskom". (Interview, August 1994.)

Eskom is in the process of trying to shift away from its historically authoritarian, paternalistic managerial practices to a more transparent, participatory culture. The Unfolding Vision constitutes a major part of this commitment to change. Senior managers at Eskom readily admitted that getting support for this process was achieving uneven success. Some mid-level white managers felt enabled by the inclusiveness of the Unfolding Vision but others seemed genuinely perplexed by employees "asking so many unnecessary questions".

However, more than half of the managers (black and white) interviewed felt that there was still a *"ja baas"* culture at Eskom. Questioning or criticising your superior meant jeopardising your chances of promotion. This was particularly the case for C Upper employees and above. One of these summarised the situation as follows:

> To get promoted, you have to be on good terms with the executive director,
> which means you don't complain, you toe the line ... if you want to get promoted.
> (Interview, August 1994.)

Eskom is aware of this problem and there are plans to ensure that the internal recruitment processes become more transparent[1].

There were also employees in other sectors who felt that Eskom's "open door policy" was effective and fair. Under this policy, all employees, irrespective of rank, can take their concerns to whatever managerial level in the organisation they wanted to. These employees tended to be between A band and C Lower. One black secretary said:

> I feel Eskom is my home. It depends on your own outlook. I can walk into (my
> manager's) office and say whatever I want to say. I don't feel threatened because
> the majority of secretaries are white in my section and I am the only black. I feel
> welcome to do as I please.

Employees from A to E band (except for some white male and female middle managers) overwhelmingly agreed that the prevalent organisational culture at Eskom was a white, male-dominated culture. This culture was not receptive to increased participation by black employees and women.

The perceptions of discrimination on the job varied by sector and business unit. In some areas, segregated facilities and racist language were still tolerated and in others the only employees with complaints about discrimination were white men. In the latter situation, the current affirmative action policy was cited as proof of this discrimination. Generally, however, there was a strong perception among employees that because of the broader socio-political changes in the country, overt discrimination was out and covert forms of discrimination were becoming more common.

Eskom is committed to on-going training for employees, as well as to the

---

1. *When asked for a definition of transparency at Eskom, one senior human resource manager replied that it meant "being able to defend the decision taken".*

development of apprentices and granting of bursaries in technically related fields. Eskom recently committed itself to ensuring all of its employees were "functionally literate" by 1996. This will address the needs of approximately 11 000 employees. It is developing a well co-ordinated Adult Basic Education (ABE) programme through which employees will be able to learn in company time and recognition will be given for prior learning. Efforts are being made to ensure line management support for the programme and accountability structures are being developed to promote the utilisation of newly learned skills. Currently, there are 1 115 employees in ABE training (ABE regional status report January-August 1994).

METHOD AND SAMPLE

Fifty three in-depth, structured, anonymous interviews (of 30 to 60 minutes long) were conducted in each of Eskom's 10 groups. Just over half of the interviews were conducted outside the corporate headquarters at Megawatt Park. The majority of the interviews were set up by Eskom human resource managers in the individual groups; the remaining interviews were conducted using a "snowball" method.

All the interviews were with employees who had been with Eskom for at least two years. When a human resource manager set up the interviews, a list was submitted requesting employees from each band level, with a particular emphasis on women employees where possible. Documentation on Eskom's history with affirmative action was requested from all employees interviewed who had, or currently have, access to such material. Much of the documentation relating to equal opportunity and affirmative action at Eskom since the mid-1980s no longer exists. Back issues of in-house news publications obtained from Eskom's library were used when possible.

Each employee interviewed was informed about the purpose of the interview and promised a copy of the chapter upon completion.

The breakdown of employees interviewed is shown in the table overleaf:

HISTORY OF AFFIRMATIVE ACTION

PILOT INITIATIVES: 1970S – 1985

Eskom's first steps towards affirmative action for black South Africans can be traced back to the early 1970s. When former chief executive Dr Ian McRae was in charge of generation at Eskom, the organisation expanded rapidly. It quickly became apparent that the supply of available skills would not keep up with the demand generated by the construction of new power stations.

McRae used these conditions as an opportunity to promote affirmative action as a growth strategy. He used economic growth as a generator for

■ TABLE 2 ■

INTERVIEW SAMPLE

BAND LEVEL	A	B	C	D	E	F	TOTAL
MEN	2	7	11	7	7	3	37
WOMEN	1	5	2	7	1	0	16
TOTAL	3	12	13	14	8	3	53

BREAKDOWN BY GENDER AND RACE

	MEN	WOMEN	TOTAL
BLACK	23	8	31
WHITE	14	8	22
TOTAL	37	16	53

BREAKDOWN BY RACE, AND BAND LEVEL

	A	B	C	D	E	F	TOTAL
BLACK	3	10	6	7	4	1	31
WHITE	0	2	7	7	4	2	22
TOTAL	3	12	13	14	8	3	53

Note: Band levels M, P and S have been collapsed into what is known as D band.

"pushing the lid off that which was keeping operators and blacks from moving up in the organisation". (Interview, August 1994.)

After a process of consultation with white unions and black power station workers, where he listened to and addressed their concerns, McRae eventually succeeded in convincing them that "everyone would gain from the growth and upward mobility opening up in the company ... this is vital: it cannot be threatening to people, people must see the opportunities for them in the plan".

A successful pilot project at one power station was launched and duplicated at other power stations. The extent of progress made at that time has been difficult to measure, particularly since, when McRae was promoted into another section of Eskom, his successor did not carry on with the programme. In addition, the changing political context in the 1970s had a significant impact on Eskom's activities.

A former Eskom corporate strategist said that from the late 1970s to the

mid-1980s, "there was no fertile soil for affirmative action – white South
Africa was retreating into the *laager*". During this period, he argued, Eskom
was caught between several cross-cutting pressures. It became part of the state
security apparatus during the "total onslaught" years and had to electrify farms
on the borders at an enormous cost to itself. Power stations and sub-stations
were targets of armed attacks and there was increased militancy from the trade
unions. He explained that, "senior blacks didn't want to be seen in Eskom
because it was seen as part of state machinery".

Nevertheless, Eskom said in the early 1980s that it was "committed to
equal opportunity within the laws of the land". In practice, this meant very
little given the rigid apartheid laws in the country at the time.

EQUAL OPPORTUNITY: 1985 – 1992

In the mid-1980s, an increase in the electricity tariff led to a tremendous
public outcry. In response, a government commission appointed John Maree as
chairperson of the Electricity Council and McRae as chief executive in 1985.
A headline in the 30 November 1985 edition of *Eskom News* said "Equal
Opportunities for all at Eskom". Interviewing McRae, the in-house publication
quoted him as saying:

> Management has long accepted the well-founded concept that productivity,
> human relations and the overall business environment in an organisation like
> ours can best be enhanced by the enjoyment of equal opportunities by all our
> employees, regardless of race, creed or sex. Eskom is committed to a non-racial
> policy and in this respect I am sure that I can count on the support of all Eskom
> employees.

While a policy is mentioned in this article, it is not possible to convey
precisely what sorts of actions or directives it contained as such documents
have not been preserved. Nevertheless, there is evidence that a series of efforts
were launched to end discriminatory practices. This included the extension of
housing subsidies to married women in 1986 and the introduction of a parity
exercise that resulted in salary increases for between 15 000 and 17 000
employees.

By 1989, according to a May 1989 *Eskom News* article, Eskom's "total
work-force of blacks, coloureds and indians (sic) in managerial positions
(made) up 58 percent of the work-force". Central motivating factors in the
development of equal opportunity in the mid-to-late 1980s were the technical
skills shortage throughout the country, coupled with political changes and
trade union pressure.

Following the announcement of equal opportunity in 1985, a programme
was developed and adopted by the board in 1991, called the "Equitable
Employment Practices and Affirmative Action Policy". With the assistance of
outside consultants, "equal opportunity entrepreneurs" were established in

each business unit to drive the process.

The equal opportunity entrepreneurs were identified by individual executive directors as employees committed to positive changes in Eskom. They were sent on training courses to enable them to identify the particular areas in their sectors that needed to be targeted in terms of making equal opportunity a success. It was a decentralised approach allowing the 65 equal opportunity entrepreneurs to design interventions appropriate to the requirements of their respective business units. Regular meetings were held at corporate headquarters with all these entrepreneurs to discuss successes and challenges.

In addition to the work of the equal opportunity entrepreneurs, forums were organised for McRae to meet a variety of staff members, listen to their concerns and answer their questions. One of the chief concerns raised in these forums by black and women employees was: Why is it that we must be appointed on experience, yet white men are appointed on potential? (Interview, August 1994.) It was an issue which Eskom attempted to address for women in the "Women in Eskom" programme.

'WOMEN IN ESKOM'

From 1986, the position of women in the work-place began receiving attention. Articles were run in the in-house newsletter discussing the barriers women faced to advancement in the work-place and the extent to which women were not given the chance to develop to their full potential.

In 1988, with the aid of an external consultant, Eskom launched a set of workshops aimed at promoting the careers and personal development of women employees. "Women in Eskom" was initially launched as a pilot project in 1987 with 350 employees, including women and their supervisors. Benefits of the workshops were listed as including:

> Improved motivation and better two-way communication between women and
> their superiors, and with both male and female colleagues. Thus productivity
> and utilisation of women workers on all levels can be promoted (*Eskom News*,
> January 1988).

Supervisors attended the first half-day of the two-day workshop to provide them with "a better understanding of the programme and of the problems facing working women" (*Eskom News*, January 1988). According to a 1988 edition of *Eskom News*, "Women in Eskom" was the biggest project of its kind to be conducted in South Africa at that time. By February 1989, 800 Eskom women employees and 350 of their managers had participated. There is no data available indicating the proportion of black and white women who attended, nor the racial and gender breakdown within Eskom as a whole at this time. An evaluation of the overall success of "Women in Eskom" was not available and very few employees who were interviewed recalled the initiative.

The programme demonstrated that trying to "workshop" discrimination out of an organisation without rigorously addressing the structures, procedures and power imbalances through which discrimination is perpetuated, has very little noticeable impact. Eskom's current gender staffing ratios seem to support this conclusion.

'NO POTENTIAL LOST'

"No Potential Lost" was a combination equal opportunity/affirmative action programme aimed at employing everyone in the company to the best of their potential. "No Potential Lost" became a separate function within the human resources department in 1989. It was first managed by a senior white male manager, then in 1990 by Eskom's first appointed E band black manager. The policy that was adopted in 1991 had two components:

EQUITABLE EMPLOYMENT PRACTICES:

- No discrimination on the grounds of inappropriate criteria.
- Job requirement standards are appropriate to the job.
- Jobs are designed on organisational requirements for labour and available skills.
- Equal reward for equal performance and market validity.
- Competent people are appointed.
- Staff are supported by development and retraining opportunities based on potential and the demand for skill.
- Eskom's work-force profile will match the skills profile of the labour market.

AFFIRMATIVE ACTION:

As the actual skills profile of the Eskom work-force does not match the skills profile in the labour market, Eskom will:
- Develop cultural synergy and common values.
- Give preference to the development of potential found in under-represented groups.
- Give preference to appointing members from all under-represented groups. (Taken from *Eskom News*, February 1991).

Specific targets were not set and compliance with the policy was largely voluntary. It was up to each sector to set its own targets, there was little formalised monitoring or evaluation and results were not formally reported. The human resources department was accountable for the programme.

The vast majority of employees interviewed (who were at Eskom during this period) recalled very little about Eskom having had an earlier equal opportunity policy. Most did not know anything similar had existed before the

1994 Affirmative Action policy. Those who were aware of it, black and white, felt that it was ineffective, having little noticeable impact on the organisation.

McRae said it was a phase "aimed at changing attitudes". He said that "at the time, we didn't really understand what we were doing with affirmative action, and there were things we did wrong, but it was necessary to go through a learning curve". (Interview, August 1994.) Problems identified by McRae included "not recognising threats on all sides, failing to recognise and put in place a coherent plan ... it bumped along, we didn't achieve really exciting progress".

A relatively significant number of black graduates were brought into the organisation in 1988. During the case study interviews, many of the black employees hired at this time recalled the trying and undermining conditions in which they were expected to perform.

One black manager said that when he started:

> I went through hell. I spent six months doing nothing but being paid at the end
> of the month. I read *The Star* until lunch. Then I slept in the afternoon. It was
> the times. I joined Eskom when we (black managers) were a test case – to see
> how black graduates would be seen in the organisation. We were the pilot
> case.

The experience of not being given work to do, and having to endure a less-than-supportive work environment, was echoed by several other black managers in various sectors hired during this period:

> When I started none of my colleagues had been told anything. The people
> weren't prepared. I was brought in and dumped amongst an unwelcoming group
> of white ladies ... there was a lot of resistance, but after time, I was accepted."
> (Interview, August 1994.)

Some of the human resource practitioners interviewed said that the blacks hired under "No Potential Lost" did help change perceptions about what black people were capable of doing. Several of the black managers hired in the late 1980s agreed with this view.

Reasons for the overall lack of results produced by the equal opportunity phase were cited as being that it was under-resourced, there was limited board commitment, hard targets were not set, and the overall environment – internally and externally – was not conducive.

HARMONISATION AND AFFIRMATIVE ACTION: 1992–1994

With the significant socio-political changes sweeping the country by 1992, Eskom decided to broaden the equal opportunity function into a newly established area within human resources called "Social Harmonisation". Different human resource managers were brought in to staff the unit, and a new senior black manager (Eskom's first black woman E band manager) was appointed to run the unit. The term "harmonisation" was developed by a consultant using McRae's dictum of "needing to always make sure Eskom is in harmony with itself and its environment".

"Social Harmonisation's" function, according to "founder members" of this unit, was to develop harmony in Eskom. This was to be done "in terms of the racial composition of the staff, the relations between labour and management and the relations between the different levels and functions in the organisation where there may have been friction in the past". It also aimed to address "external harmonisation with the communities in which we do business, listening to their needs, building relationships, assisting them to develop themselves through education support programmes, and the electrification of schools and clinics..." (Interviews, September 1994.)

While affirmative action was part of the internal social harmonisation process, initially it did not receive as much attention as the external harmonisation processes of developing community links and promoting social development projects. This created some friction within the organisation as many employees – black and white – felt "harmonisation" was a glossing over of the need for affirmative action in Eskom itself. Some black managers said they had been very frustrated when Eskom received recognition for its external affirmative action efforts when very little seemed to be changing internally.

However, other managers interviewed (black and white) pointed out that Eskom's reputation as a business leader in the affirmative action arena intensified the pressure on the leadership to live up to its image.

Under "Social Harmonisation", the promotion and placement of senior black employees did receive increased attention. Issues that had, until then, largely been ignored in relation to affirmative action began to demand attention. In particular, the work environment in which black employees were expected to perform was now recognised as a significant contributing factor to the loss of black talent.

A senior black human resources manager said:

> We recognised that the "revolving door syndrome" was occurring because the organisation was not prepared within ... There was nothing to help you settle in when you came here, into a hostile environment. We needed to support one another. The only way to deal with it was to be tough skinned and (the Black Consultative Forum) was there to be supportive. (Interview, September 1994.)

THE BLACK CONSULTATIVE FORUM

The Black Consultative Forum (BCF) was launched in 1992. It was closely linked to the "Social Harmonisation" department. It provided a forum for black managers (the equivalent of D band and above) to "speak as a collective to management about our lack of involvement – especially in the macro issues – because we are all spread so thin throughout the organisation". (Interview with BCF founder member, September 1994.)

The specific purpose of the BCF is a contentious issue among some black managers, particularly since it began receiving funding from Eskom itself. The BCF now has approximately 100 members and meets quarterly.

BCF conducted a study into why black professionals had been leaving Eskom in large numbers during the previous two to three years. It was discovered that none left exclusively because they wanted better salaries elsewhere:

> Their complaints were that their jobs had been watered down, they were not
> being given enough responsibility, whites were refusing to report to them ... it
> had to do with the environment". (Interview, August 1994.)

Through the lobbying efforts of the BCF, the harmonisation department, and other observant human resource managers, it was recognised that a more rigorous approach to affirmative action was needed.

"Playing with words and hiding behind equal opportunity was not going to get us anywhere," said one senior human resources manager. Another added that equal opportunity and social harmonisation had "assisted us in making the paradigm shift from equal opportunity to affirmative action ... it showed the limitations of not attacking things vigorously". More specifically, "the previous efforts did not directly take into account the ways in which South Africa's history has disproportionately disadvantaged the majority of its people ... we needed to tackle this head-on and stop pussy-footing around". (Interview, September 1994.)

In addition, there was concern that current approaches to affirmative action were not delivering quickly enough to allow Eskom to keep up with its changing customer base as well as political changes in the country.

A combination of external political and economic pressures combined with pressure being exerted from within the organisation contributed to Eskom committing itself to a bolder approach to affirmative action. This would be visibly driven by the management board and would include set targets.

DEVELOPING AN AFFIRMATIVE ACTION POLICY

The social harmonisation department was charged with developing a more refined and vigorous affirmative action policy. It began by consulting all the political organisations and asking for policy statements on affirmative action. Organisations such as the South African Chamber of Business, the Black Management Forum and 20 South African companies were contacted for their positions on affirmative action. Internally, the BCF and Eskom's 11 trade unions were consulted. There was, however, a discrepancy between the views of trade union representatives and those of Eskom management interviewed about the extent and timing of this consultation.

After consultation, an affirmative action project team representing various viewpoints was formed in the harmonisation department. According to human resource managers involved in the process, an organisational culture audit was not conducted, nor was there a thorough evaluation of past equal opportunity/ affirmative action programmes. External consultants were brought in, literature was reviewed and some project team members went on a fact-finding tour to the United States. Issues were vigorously debated until a document was produced.

Some of the main areas of disagreement included: the position of white women in relation to the policy, promotion opportunities for white men and alternative job creation initiatives.

After the project team reached agreement, the draft was taken around individually to each executive director for comment, with the understanding that their comments "would not necessarily be incorporated". (Interview, July 1994.) These were brought back to the project team who tried to reconcile the various concerns. One team member said "in some cases, (the concerns) conflicted quite badly".

Before presenting the final product to the management board, the document was presented to the trade unions. It was received with mixed reactions but only one union, the white, right-wing Mine Workers' Union, was vehemently against it. Its objections to the document were noted at every presentation thereafter.

ESKOM'S STANCE ON AFFIRMATIVE ACTION

CURRENT POLICY AND IMPLEMENTATION

A document entitled *Eskom's Stance on Affirmative Action* was formally adopted by the management board of Eskom on 16 February 1994. In this document, Eskom committed itself to:

> Transform the demographic profile of our business so as to more realistically reflect the community in which we conduct our business. This is a key business priority ... key performance indicators will be set and progress in meeting them will be measured.

The "desired end state" of affirmative action spelled out by the document is to reach a stage where:
- Race, gender and creed have no effect on employment opportunities.
- Eskom values and cherishes its cultural diversity.
- Performance and ability are the only criteria by which employees and potential employees are judged.
- Eskom is viewed as having credibility and legitimacy.

Targets were set for changing the demographic profile of Eskom's staff. These were incorporated into each executive director's performance contract.

Thirty percent of all staff in C Upper positions to F band levels on the Paterson grading system had to be black South Africans by the year 1996 and 50 percent by the year 2000. "Black" was defined as including coloured and Asian people. White women were not considered primary beneficiaries of affirmative action. The policy stated, however, that "the company is ... addressing gender inequality by opening up opportunities for women of all races to enjoy the same benefits as men".

Key features of *Eskom's Stance on Affirmative Action* include:

- Recognising the effects of past discriminatory practices and the barriers these created against black South Africans.
- Ensuring that affirmative action is seen as a means to an end.
- Introducing a strategy, policies and practices aimed at altering the racial and gender profile of Eskom to be more representative of the nation as a whole.
- Supporting black South African small business and encouraging the companies with which it does business to do the same.
- Removing any remaining discriminatory practices regarding equality of employment.

In order to meet its targets and achieve the goals it has set for itself, Eskom gives preference to black bursars and trainees and to black staff for promotions and job applicants. If a more experienced white person and a black person apply for the same job from inside or outside the company, the black person must be given priority. He or she must meet the basic qualifications required for the job, with an emphasis being placed on potential rather than on experience.

The policy document says: "No white employee will lose his (sic) job in Eskom as a result of affirmative action." It adds, however, that "as part of space creation initiatives, white employees may not necessarily remain in their present portfolios/jobs. Any movement of staff will be done in a fair and equitable manner and in consultation with the affected employees". There is no automatic early retirement; individual employees must negotiate on a one-to-one basis with their appropriate managers for a severance package, which at the moment ranges from two to five months' pay.

The document recognises that there may be attempts to disrupt the affirmative action process, and states that these "will not be tolerated ... (We) recognise however that there may be some resistance to this programme. (We) are determined to overcome resistance through consultation and reassurance and by stressing the business imperative".

It is up to each of the 10 executive directors to decide the extent to which the required targets will be incorporated into line managers' performance appraisals. In practice most line managers negotiate specific targets with their general managers. Executive directors are not given a specific budget for implementing affirmative action or for developing existing talent because it is believed that this will force managers to use the black employees they hire efficiently rather than "hiring faces who sit and do nothing all day". (Interview, August 1994.).

There are many senior managers who believe that there is still a lot of "dead wood" in the organisation. Meeting the affirmative action targets within existing budgets will compel them to ensure that every employee is performing efficiently.

As a separate, but complementary, goal every Eskom employee is to have a personal development plan (PDP) which s/he develops with his or her supervisor. The PDP provides an opportunity for managers to assess existing under-utilised talent, as well as to identify areas that are "over-resourced".

The affirmative action policy was introduced to managers through what several human resource managers throughout Eskom referred to as a "roadshow". It was led by a team from the harmonisation department who were present when the policy was introduced by the highest ranking managers in each area to his/her managers.

After the introduction, the stance document was handed out to all the managers present, who were in turn to introduce and distribute the policy among their lower-level supervisors and employees. In theory, every employee of Eskom should have a copy of *Eskom's Stance on Affirmative Action* and be aware of what it entails.

Top management is aware that not all employees, particularly at A and B band levels, have received information about affirmative action. This is perceived by management to be the result of a lack of co-operation by line managers. Many white line managers interviewed complained of not understanding enough about the policy to explain it to their workers. One white union representative recalled how, at the roadshows, "people were too intimidated to ask questions ... it was made clear that if you asked questions you would be in trouble ..." (Interview, July 1994.) As a result, some managers do not know how to answer the questions asked by their subordinates.

There were, however, some sectors of Eskom where the senior levels of management went to great lengths to "prepare the ground in advance" for the introduction of the affirmative action policy. In at least one area, a video was prepared by the senior manager explaining why the coming changes had to happen and he invited employees to speak to him about their concerns. Positive outcomes arising from this effort were reported by a variety of employees interviewed in this sector.

There is tension in the human resource sectors as to whether a strong "rhino" approach to affirmative action would be more effective, or if the "softly, softly" approach of the past would be wiser in the long term. These opposing perspectives, interestingly, are not divided along racial lines.

Specific strengths of the current affirmative action policy most frequently mentioned in the interviews included: the existence of a policy with targets and accountability structures; the appointment of three black executive directors to the management board; the appointment of a black power station manager. Areas still being worked on include "making the cost of non-compliance visible" and developing creative mechanisms to deal with persistent covert discrimination within the organisation. More specifically, several senior human resource managers are concerned that the affirmative action programme is being interpreted simply as a numbers game.

One manager said: "Out of 100 percent, there is about a 98 percent focus on targets and numbers, and yet 98 percent of the problems are not about numbers." One of the most critical challenges seen to be facing Eskom's affirmative action programme was changing the work-place environment. Many employees interviewed (from A to F band) recognised this as a crucial factor in shaping Eskom's ability to succeed with affirmative action. Moreover, many of these same employees perceived a direct link between changing Eskom's work environment and the long term possibility of Eskom remaining an innovative organisation well into the 21st century.

Senior human resource managers interviewed said that addressing the issues of changing the work-place environment required "a multi-dimensional view of affirmative action" which was constrained by numbers game perceptions. Such a view would emphasise the inter-relatedness of the work environment and human resource practices. Related to this is communication throughout the organisation of what affirmative action means in both the macro and micro contexts, and how employees' concerns regarding affirmative action are being addressed.

The "multi-dimensional view of affirmative action" would attempt to shift the focus of affirmative action away from numbers to recognising what Eskom had learned from its experiences and what it still needed to learn. Some senior human resource managers said that managers at all levels needed to learn to think of affirmative action "more like a relay race instead of a sprint ... we need to think like long distance runners. If you move too quickly you will mess people up ... there are critical decisions that have to be made (in every sphere) ... You have to get a balance so there is excitement, tension and progress ..." (Interview, October 1994.)

EVALUATION OF THE POLICY

AFFIRMATIVE ACTION IS A 'HARD' ISSUE

Eskom's evolving experiences with affirmative action suggest that it is more effective, as well as cost effective, to deal with affirmative action directly, with hard targets and direct language. The past policies that had no targets, no evaluation procedures and where accountability lay with the human resources department instead of the board, produced few exciting results. Eskom's experience teaches that affirmative action must be dealt with both as a business imperative and as a matter of economic survival, not as an act of charity.

In pursuing affirmative action as a business imperative fully integrated into key performance indicators, factors that are likely to impede the overall success of affirmative action must be identified and addressed. Eskom is working on this, though there is a great deal of disagreement over the extent to which punitive action should be taken in response to non-compliance. Withholding an annual bonus is not necessarily going to halt covert racist practices when the only factor being evaluated is the number of black employees in a department. It is more likely to simply drive racist behaviour underground, leaving it to seep out in more deceptive ways.

Non-compliance with any aspect of the affirmative action policy, including the promotion of a non-discriminatory work-place environment, should be treated with the same seriousness as other cases of non-compliance or resistance to other business imperatives.

Similarly, the decisions on which staff members should oversee the affirmative action policy development and implementation process, should be made with particular sensitivity. An employee who has worked in human resources for many years is not necessarily competent to handle the myriad of issues involved in affirmative action.

A SUPPORTIVE ENVIRONMENT FOR AFFIRMATIVE ACTION

The experiences at Eskom indicated that the work environment cannot be overlooked in the development and implementation of an affirmative action policy. An affirmative action impact analysis, to determine where the main changes and barriers to change would lie in developing and implementing affirmative action, was never conducted at Eskom. At the time of this research the human resources department at Megawatt Park was in the process of offering to conduct organisational culture audits for the individual business units.

Yet a gap still remains in the dissemination of information and communication within the individual business units, and Eskom as a whole, as to what affirmative action means in theory and in practice. There are many conflicting interpretations of what is supposed to change in the organisation, in what manner, and how quickly these changes should happen. There are rumours circulating which undermine the creation of a supportive environment for affirmative action.

Eskom's experience suggests that, in attempting to implement a strategy as multifaceted as affirmative action, it must be recognised that emotions are already running high in the changed socio-political situation in South Africa. The results of a failure to disseminate accurate information about affirmative action, as well as resistance from many line managers to change, must not be overlooked but rather taken as a starting point.

One of the biggest challenges senior human resource managers identified was the creation of mechanisms to help line managers to achieve affirmative action goals. Part of this would involve identifying threats and fears and turning these into opportunities. One lesson identified is the importance of ensuring that all employees understand why affirmative action is necessary. They must also understand that it can benefit everyone in the organisation (and the country) if it succeeds. Moreover, it is vital for each employee to understand that they have a role to play in the process of affirmative action and in securing the organisation's future economic success.

Eskom recognises that the incorporation of affirmative action goals, not just targets, into all human resource practices can help substantially in creating a supportive environment for affirmative action. At the moment they are exploring the creation of a user-friendly grievance mechanism to address discriminatory behaviour and practices within the institution swiftly and transparently[2]. Other suggestions included consulting employees about what they think are the main issues hindering the creation of a supportive, non-discriminatory work environment and possible ways of addressing these issues. Many general workers interviewed suggested organising more sporting events for employees as one possible way to start breaking down communication barriers. In terms of addressing white employees' concerns and fears, suggestions included developing alternative remuneration schemes, such as regular overseas trips, and creating more lateral movement opportunities.

Many senior managers at Eskom recognise the importance of developing innovative and creative human resource practices to cultivate a sustainable supportive work-place environment for all its employees. This need is not being viewed in a vacuum separately from other aspects of the organisation's daily functioning. New human resource practices which help establish a lasting supportive work environment for affirmative action are viewed as being closely linked to the overall continued success of Eskom as a company.

TRAINING AND DEVELOPMENT

Eskom's commitment to the training and development of its staff is admirable. In addition to ABE provisions, and the support of black bursars and apprentices, Eskom is developing its future leaders (black and white) through its three-year accelerated development or management training programme. The largest portion of the training budget, however, is allocated to keeping the more senior technological areas abreast of global technological changes. Most people in these areas are white men, and they tend to receive a dis-

---

2. *Currently, Eskom is trying to address this issue through "Understanding Racism" and "Managing Diversity" workshops, with mixed success. There is a great deal of resistance to these workshops from white staff in particular, and in some cases the workshops are promoting the opposite of what was intended. "Now we know how much and why the blacks hate us," was the way one white employee summed up her understanding of the workshop. (Interview, September 1994.) Some senior human resource managers question the long-term benefits of the workshops. They are conducted outside the office environment and away from colleagues; employees go through three days of intensely personal training only to go back to an un-changed office environment.*

proportionate amount of the training budget.

Eskom's present affirmative action policy does not disaggregate the manner in which all executives must meet their targets. Thus the historically "soft" areas of Eskom's business units tend to experience an increase in black employees and the "technical" areas have remained largely white and male. A significant constraint in this area is that the power stations tend to be right-wing strongholds. There is a reluctance on the part of many white employees to provide on-the-job training to black colleagues who they see as direct threats to their livelihoods.

It was acknowledged by some of the human resource managers interviewed that there were problems with black employees receiving training and not being given the opportunity to put their new skills into practice. This was seen as an obstacle to the upward mobility of black and women employees throughout Eskom. Many black employees interviewed, from A to E band, referred to not being allowed to take risks, learn from their mistakes and develop from hands-on experience.

The need to articulate training and development with affirmative action is frequently overlooked when training and development strategies are formulated. It is also a major hidden barrier to "growing talent" within an organisation when white technicians and/or managers obstruct black and women employees in practising and developing the skills required for promotion.

Eskom has recognised the need to monitor this problem in its current ABE plans by ensuring that skills learned in ABE are used on the job. However, there is a need for this type of monitoring to occur on a broader basis to ensure that all black and women employees are encouraged and allowed to use the skills developed in training. Innovative targets need to be developed which allocate responsibility not simply for the hiring or promotion of black employees, but for the promotion of hands-on skill development opportunities. This is of vital importance in technical areas where there are significantly fewer black employees than in the administrative, human resources, marketing and/or public relations related sectors.

Moreover, there is a serious need for a job skills audit to match existing skills and potential within the organisation with changing business demands. The issue of under-utilisation of skills of existing staff has generally not been given serious attention at the business unit level. Under apartheid many blacks lied about their work-related skills so that they were not "over-qualified" for menial jobs on offer. A job skills audit could therefore be very fruitful. The personal development plans do provide such a way to address these issues, but there is no procedure to ensure that they are used in this particular manner.

The decentralisation of Eskom provides the latitude for managers to provide better customer service. In terms of integrating overall affirmative action requirements into existing human resource practices, however, a major gap persists in many areas.

Eskom has increased the proportion of black bursars and apprentices it funds but it still has obligations to offer employment to existing white bursars, who still outnumber black bursars. Solutions need to be found to ensure that the commitment to white bursar holders does not prevent Eskom from reaching the affirmative action targets set. Ultimately, linking affirmative action with training and development depends on being flexible and creative in integrating affirmative action with human resource practices.

EMPLOYEE PARTICIPATION

Eskom has learned from experience that clear communication with employees on affirmative action issues is vital. Its most recent experience with the development of the 1994 affirmative action document further emphasised the importance of meaningful consultation in the policy development and implementation process.

Despite Eskom's efforts to consult with a wide range of groups, very few non-human resources employees thought the formulation of the document had been sufficiently participatory or consultative. Some human resource managers suggested that in-house media could have been more effectively used throughout the development and implementation process. This could have aided in the development of a common understanding of what affirmative action meant for the company, for each department, for the company's relationship with stakeholders as well as for the individual employee.

This suggests that involving as many people as possible in getting to grips with, developing and implementing affirmative action could significantly reduce the tendency for it to be seen as an exclusively black (or even anti-white) issue.

Some senior human resource managers suggested, with hindsight, that a more thorough participatory process could also have further emphasised board commitment to affirmative action. This could have been done by creating forums where these issues were discussed. This approach, where regular discussion/report-back sessions are held in non-threatening environments, could also help to reach the large proportion of Eskom employees who are not union members. This would allow them to stay abreast of the development process as well as to voice their concerns.

They also pointed out the need for participation to be linked to tolerance. Effective participation takes time, but it is an opportunity for all involved to listen to one another. It can be very frustrating and unproductive for everyone if it is not structured carefully, with agreed ground rules or principles.

CONCLUSION

The evolution of affirmative action at Eskom has not been a smooth, unfolding process. Eskom's history as a parastatal played a role in the shifting approaches taken towards affirmative action, as did social, political and economic forces both inside and outside the organisation.

Central learning points from Eskom's experiences with affirmative action include the fact that affirmative action must not be seen as a product but rather as a process that requires significant time, attention, participation and communication throughout the organisation. Its success is closely linked to the building of a supportive work-place environment. Successfully integrating affirmative action goals into human resource practices can help shape an appropriate work-place environment. Moreover, Eskom's experiences strongly indicate that affirmative action needs to be driven by a dedicated management board whose support for the programme is clearly visible. ■

UNIVERSITY OF THE WESTERN CAPE

PELIWE LOLWANA,
JEANNE GAMBLE AND
WARREN KRAFCHIK

PROFILE OF THE UNIVERSITY[1]

The University of the Western Cape (UWC) has a long and active tradition of struggle against apartheid. Its agenda has been one of radical transformation, with affirmative action being seen as an important component in this process.

A statement by Archbishop Desmond Tutu, chancellor of the university, during an interview with the *Financial Mail* in 1993, perhaps best captures the spirit of transformation:

> UWC was spawned by apartheid as an ethnic coloured bush college. But the people decided to take it over, to transform it into a university that was no ivory tower but one responsive to, and serving the interests of, the community of apartheid's victims.

UWC was established in 1960, under the Extension of University Education Act, to provide residential tertiary education for people classified as coloured. It could therefore be argued that, under apartheid, UWC had an affirmative action agenda for a particular race group from the beginning. In a document entitled "The History of the University of the Western Cape", Professor Nicky Morgan, however, reminds us that the institution was rejected by the community, shunned and scorned by black academics and attended under protest by most of its students. Faculties were dominated by conservative, white Afrikaners and during the first 10 years only three black staff appointments were made at junior levels. Lunch time extension lectures

---

1. *This section draws on the following documents: "A vital role player in the new SA,"* Financial Mail, *12 February 1993: 59-72; Morgan, N. 1989. "The history of the University of the Western Cape."* UWC Student Orientation Guide.

organised by the administration to win the "hearts and minds" of students, included topics such as "The Dangers of Communism".

During most of the 1960s, the university was politically silent. The first direct challenge to the university authorities was in 1970 when students protested against the formal dress code in a tie-burning ceremony. Subsequent structural grievances included restrictive university rules, hostel problems such as food and visiting hours, the composition of council where the community was not represented, an administration that implemented separate amenities and a refusal by the administration to recognise the Student Representative Council (SRC) constitution.

These protests on pressing campus issues coincided with the re-emergence of country-wide resistance among workers and students against repressive and undemocratic work-place and education practices[2].

In line with the government's philosophy of separate development for different race or ethnic groups, Professor Richard van der Ross was appointed as the first coloured rector in 1975. This change in leadership, however, heralded a new era in the university's history, characterised by the creation of the space for dissent.

Rather than resorting to the confrontational strategies of the previous administration, the university authorities embarked upon a route of consultation and negotiation, despite the difficulties encountered. Gradually, conservative, white and coloured academic and administrative staff appointed by the government during the apartheid era were either transformed or marginalised. Some took advantage of a clause in the Associated Institutions Pensions Act and took early retirement on the grounds that the circumstances of their employment had changed fundamentally. This allowed for the appointment of more progressive staff to senior positions.

In 1982, the council of the university formally rejected the ideological reason for the university's establishment. Instead of UWC becoming a tertiary institution for coloureds only, council officially committed the university to "the development of Third World communities in southern Africa". Admissions policies were changed and anyone with the statutory minimum qualification who applied was admitted, except in a few specialised areas, such as dentistry[3].

Since 1990, UWC has been offering first year places to all applicants with an A or B matric aggregate. It then allocates 80 percent of the places on a random basis, drawing on a pool of applicants with the basic minimum pass.

In 1987, Professor Jakes Gerwel, a graduate of UWC and a former staff member, was appointed as rector. Although the student population had doubled, the spirit of militancy and resistance continued and the university's transformation agenda remained a high priority. He reiterated the aim of

---

2. *The 1976 Soweto schools crisis typifies the mood and activism of the times.*
3. *The backlog at this stage was huge and even by 1992 national statistics still showed that whereas 35 out of every 1 000 whites were at university, the corresponding number for blacks was six or seven.*

making UWC a "people's university" and declared in his inaugural speech that UWC was consciously aiming to be "the intellectual home of the left".

Despite the withdrawal of some donor support and a degree of cultural intolerance because of the rapid change in the composition of the student population, UWC is determined to be truly non-racist and non-sexist. In this it hopes to serve as a model for the broader South African society. Research on student selection is ongoing and the university is proud of the statistics that show that, by 1994, UWC had approximately 46 percent African students, as opposed to 1 percent 10 years before.

An academic development programme for both staff and students has done important pioneering work in the teaching of previously disadvantaged students while maintaining academic standards. The university is also trying to develop a satisfactory response to the need to make English the lingua franca of UWC. Many students speak Afrikaans or an African language. The language policy project is, according to Professor Renfrew Christie, dean of research at UWC, "a living experiment, coping with a range of languages from Arabic to Zulu".

The staff composition has, not unexpectedly, continued to change over the years. Academic staff are drawn from the UWC graduate population, as well as from other South African universities and abroad. South Africans who went into exile and who built academic reputations abroad are also returning to teach and to conduct research at UWC. While UWC's research capacity cannot yet be compared with some of the other long-established universities, the recently established University Development Programme is seen as a deliberate effort to develop the sciences at the historically black universities. Post-graduate activity, a good indicator of research capacity, has risen markedly. The number of honours degrees awarded increased from 90 in 1986 to 196 in 1991, while masters and doctoral degrees rose from 11 to 46 in the same period.

Clearly, since the university's autonomy was granted in 1983, much has been done to achieve academic excellence. At the same time, it has provided access to students who would not normally gain entry to a university. Issues such as racism and sexism are integral curriculum components across faculties as the university works actively towards broader societal transformation and empowerment through community partnerships. The dentistry school and hospital, for instance, have been moved to Mitchells Plain, a coloured residential area outside Cape Town, from where they serve at least 30 000 patients from Mitchells Plain and the African townships of Guguletu, Nyanga and Khayelitsha, a total community of about two million people. The education faculty provides in-service teacher training and the Goldfields Research Centre aims to improve the literacy of township children during the first three years of schooling. The law faculty offers a legal aid clinic, complemented by a street law project and community law centre that aims to make citizens aware of their legal rights and duties.

Gerwel, who subsequently left the university to work in the President's

Office, should perhaps have the final word in this section:

> As for affirmative action, this should not be mechanical. In appointing staff our
> first duty is to enhance the intellectual quality of the university. But we must
> also attend to social empowerment, to careful development. In both areas we
> have a specific sympathy for previously exiled academics. As for the
> composition of the staff, we are doing well with the racial balance but not with
> gender equality. We will continue to work for a fair balance between people from
> urban and rural origin — and do our best to ensure that working-class people
> have access." (*Financial Mail*, February 1993)

This case study will concentrate on gender equity, within a broader
framework of transformational initiatives. UWC is the only institution in the
research sample that is tackling these issues in a consistent and formalised
manner. Gender equity is treated as an issue in its own right, rather than as
something that is added on to affirmative action policies in a "politically
correct" manner without much being done to address its particular problems
and barriers. Organisations that decide to address the issue of gender equity
openly and directly will learn a great deal from the UWC experience, but the
case study also provides valuable guidelines for affirmative action.

■ TABLE 1 ■

STAFF PROFILE 1994

	MALE				FEMALE				
	W	C	AS	A	W	C	AS	A	Total
PROFESSORS	25	9	-	7	4	-	-	1	46
ASSOCIATE PROFESSORS	7	5	-	1	2	2	-	-	17
SENIOR LECTURERS	33	38	1	7	20	7	-	1	107
LECTURERS	46	62	7	4	42	43	2	4	210
JUNIOR LECTURERS	8	19	2	3	21	21	3	4	81
GENERAL ADMIN	17	444	6	45	5	307	22	11	857
TOTAL	136	577	16	67	94	380	27	21	

Source: Gender Equity Unit

HISTORY OF GENDER EQUITY[4]

Formal attempts to secure gender equity at UWC began in 1987, the year that Gerwel was appointed rector. These efforts led to the creation of two voluntary groups. The first was geared to address gender issues at the level of conditions of service and the second attempted to push gender issues at a theoretical and teaching level.

WOMEN'S COMMISSION

The Women's Commission, formed in 1987, was a cross-representational alliance of members drawn from a wide range of groups. The commission's first project was to document all the blatant instances of discrimination on the campus as reflected in the policies and practices. Through negotiations with the university administration, the commission managed to secure significant changes in the conditions of work for women employees.

These early victories included the extension of maternity benefits, the establishment of a preschool for employees' children and the granting of a housing subsidy for married women. In addition, the commission secured the right of women to act as chief exam invigilators. Women had previously been excluded from this position on the spurious grounds that they were unable to carry heavy exam scripts.

After these initial gains, the commission began exploring the more subtle forms of discrimination on campus. At this point it began to appreciate the additional need for formal university structures to challenge sexism and promote women's development on campus.

WOMEN'S STUDIES GROUP

The Women's Studies Group (WSG), also formed in 1987, sought to influence university policy through intellectual and cultural programmes. The group wanted to create an awareness and debate around gender issues on campus, including the incorporation of gender issues and women's studies into the academic curriculum. The regular activities of the WSG include public meetings, debates, distribution of accessible resources on topical issues related to women and gender and the establishment of an advice centre.

ANTI-SEXUAL HARASSMENT COMMITTEE

The open debate around sexual violence and harassment at UWC was sparked

---

4. *This section draws on the following documents: Kadalie, R. 1993. "Report on initiatives taken at UWC to address discrimination against women," and Kadalie, R. 1994. "Report to Gender Policy Action Committee."*

off by a 1989 anthropological thesis on sexual harassment and rape at the university which focused particularly on the situation in the residences. The thesis raised the difficulties of dealing with sexual violence on campus in the absence of formal structures.

At the time, sexual violence was generally not considered to be a serious issue on campus. A common view was that sexual violence was endemic to society, in particular to apartheid. It was neither appropriate nor possible to effectively challenge the issue on campus. Initial opposition to the development of the debate on campus ranged from indifference to tearing down posters attempting to generate awareness.

In response to conditions in the residences and spurred on by the above-mentioned thesis, a group of residence students formed a broad-based committee, the Anti-Sexual Harassment Committee (ASHC), with members from the student body, residences and administration and academic staff. The committee worked with the WSG and the student counselling department on programmes designed to operate at two levels. The first focus was on practical steps to improve the safety of women on campus. Projects included additional locks in residences, improved lighting on campus and the removal of bushes. Later projects attempted to target and change gender consciousness on the campus through a variety of educational and cultural programmes.

After evaluating the impact of these programmes, the ASHC acknowledged the urgent need for a formal policy and intervention on sexual harassment on campus. As a start to this process, the WSG worked with the university lawyers to draft a university policy on sexual harassment. Although this version of the policy was never passed by the senate, it provided an initial input from which later developments were to benefit.

Two related initiatives established support structures on which the policy would eventually rely. The WSG compiled a resource booklet on sexual harassment and rape and translated it into Xhosa. Further, a training programme for peer councillors was introduced leading to the establishment of a women's crisis resource centre.

GENDER POLICY AND PROGRAMME OF ACTION TASK GROUP

Following pressure from two women academics on the senate academic planning committee, the Gender Policy and Programme of Action Task Group (GPPATG) was established as a sub-committee in an attempt to formalise gender activities on campus. The formation of the GPPATG represented a significant shift as it was the first formal recognition of the importance of gender issues on campus.

The GPPATG was established as a temporary body charged with two primary tasks. The first was to set the terms of reference for a permanent senate/council standing committee on gender issues, to be called the Gender Policy Action Committee (GPAC). The second task was to appoint a gender equity officer in the Gender Equity Unit (GEU) to co-ordinate gender activities on campus. GPPATG also initiated a couple of projects, such as the development of guidelines for the use of non-sexist language, which was adopted by the senate in December 1994.

The GPAC was made up of high-level staff as well as student and trade union representatives who were nominated onto the committee. The GEU, which reported directly to the rector, was staffed in a similar way. The gender co-ordinator, who was appointed, was an established academic who had been internally groomed and who had high political credibility in her own right. This ensured that the position had both high status and high stature. The co-ordinator was provided with research and administrative support and was given access to all university committee structures as well as to existing statistical data.

The GEU ensured that its working group structures included broad representation of all campus constituencies and that it continued the UWC tradition of community partnerships. The GEU also actively collaborated with similar structures on other campuses and further afield – both locally and internationally.

GENDER POLICY ACTION COMMITTEE

The GPAC includes broad representation from all stakeholders on campus in a mix that includes the strategic positions of power as well as the diversity inherent in the institution. Committee members include the rector, registrar, council, union and student representatives and the gender equity officer. The majority of the committee members must be women.

The major tasks of the committee are to:
- Review the position of women in UWC employment, including their representation on all structures and committees.
- Review the progress and obstacles facing women students at the university.
- Continually review the policies and practices at UWC, especially as they affect the social conditions of women on the campus.
- Develop gender issues and women's studies academic curricula across disciplines.
- Report regularly to the rector and the registrar.

GENDER EQUITY OFFICER

The gender equity officer was appointed in 1993. The officer's role was to "co-ordinate the implementation and the development of the university's gender policy and programme of action ... (working) ... closely with other initiatives on and off campus". The gender equity officer is to implement the aims and objectives of the GPAC and it is to this body that the co-ordinator reports on a quarterly basis.

The GEU develops the work of the GPAC. In the two years since its inception, however, it has initiated and developed a far wider range of projects than envisaged. The unit has become a home for gender issues and concerns on campus. A review of some of the programmes of the unit will convey something of the range and scope of its activities and a sense of its developing impact on campus.

A researcher was appointed to compile a statistical database of the entire work-force in 1993. Despite some initial problems with data collection, the database currently covers the faculties, research institutes, library and senate committees. Once the data covers the entire campus, it will be woven into a detailed analysis of the position of women employees on the campus.

When the unit was established, a range of problems plagued the disciplinary process surrounding sexual harassment and rape cases in the student disciplinary court. There were numerous delays in trials, a lack of consistency in applying principles and sentences and little action was seen to be taken against offenders. Following a concerted campaign by the gender equity officer, residence director and deputy registrar, the set of procedures and policies governing these matters were significantly overhauled. Some important examples of changes include:

- A student disciplinary committee has been established consisting of law professors and non-legal representatives such as the gender equity officer and members of the residence administration.
- A full-time proctor was employed in January 1995 to hear cases.
- Sentences have been standardised and strengthened to include expulsion.
- The names of offenders are published.

Following these changes, the gender equity officer reports that there has been a definite increase in the number of cases brought before the court, greater regularity in hearings, greater consistency in sentencing and harsher penalties. In turn, these developments have lead to increased confidence among students in the system and willingness to lay charges.

A number of developments spearheaded by the GEU and the co-ordinator have integrated women's studies into campus courses. In 1994, an honours course on "Women and Development" was offered within the Institute for Social Development. A women's studies Masters programme was also offered from January 1995, with courses offered jointly by lecturers from UWC and the Universities of Missouri, USA and Utrecht, the Netherlands. A winter school offered, for the first time, courses in women's studies to a broad range of women from the community. In addition, an international exchange programme, run by the GEU, develops UWC women academics through links with universities in the United States and the Netherlands. A GEU representative sits on all strategic committees including selection committees, senate committees and the human resources committee.

The unit is very active in running gender awareness and affirmative action workshops in all departments on campus and at institutions off campus. It has become a site where staff and students seek assistance on grievances and mediation. At a cultural level, the unit regularly stages relevant theatre, International Women's Day events and dance performances. A recently initiated research project, under the gender equity officer, will investigate the low proportion of women graduates moving on to graduate studies.

EVALUATION OF THE POLICY

UWC's efforts to achieve gender equity need to be interpreted within the broader university context of transformation and empowerment outlined in the first section. The campus culture has long been one of resistance and activism. Given also that a number of the more radical academics are women who work within the intellectual disciplines of women's and/or feminist studies, it was almost inevitable that women's issues would be taken up.

These two traditions came together to establish a voluntary grassroots movement that mobilised women from all sectors of campus life. Attention was simultaneously paid to both the practical and the ideological, thereby providing a range of activity options. Some women who, for instance, did not consider themselves "politically" active, felt strongly about the improvement of their basic conditions of service. Some were mobilised by the need to expose and address sexual harassment on campus; others worked to create campus awareness of women's issues. A further group aimed to introduce a consciousness and deeper theoretical perspective into curricula across faculties as well as develop a specialised area of study. Different entry points were therefore provided and coalitions across a broad range of structures – ranging from the SRC to residence administration, campus control, trade unions and staff associations – became possible.

The crucial role played by the rector in supporting and encouraging the process should also be underscored. Organisations often tend to view informal lobbying negatively, but, in this instance, the rector and registrar channelled the momentum by actively creating space for debate and policy development within formal university structures.

It is important to remind ourselves of the trajectory of the developments outlined in section two. Although the approach was broad in focus, the first initiatives involved conditions of service. Issues such as maternity benefits, housing subsidies for married women and a preschool for the children of UWC staff materially contributed towards creating a milieu where women's work was accorded equal value in monetary terms.

Such a milieu also explicitly recognised women's biological role as child bearers. An environment was also created where parental obligations of both women and men were recognised and woven into the fabric of campus society. It was recognised that parents worrying about their children and how they were being cared for interfered with their work. Many men on campus supported these moves, either on principle or because they had wives who worked under similar conditions elsewhere.

At the same time, the campus community was drawn into debates on issues like sexual harassment, rape, abortion and women's rights. Raising awareness of these issues was, however, not deemed to be sufficient in itself and practical measures were taken to establish a support system for women. This included resource and counselling centres with trained counsellors and conflict mediation services that made it easier for women to talk about matters that society still suppressed or ridiculed. Women were provided with information and advice to help them establish whether they had an arguable case and where they should lodge such a case.

Challenging the university structures and arguing for the inclusion of more women on strategic committees followed, but again not without creating spaces for women to develop themselves intellectually. This was done through study groups and international exchange programmes, as well as through informal mentoring and networking.

LESSONS FOR AFFIRMATIVE ACTION

Setting up a separate committee and an operational unit to promote gender equity raises similar problems to those experienced when setting up a separate affirmative action committee. The risk is that the issue is isolated and always treated as a special matter, rather than as something that is integrated into the human resource development practices of the organisation.

UWC overcomes this problem by integrating gender equity into all strategic structures on campus and by providing sufficient resources for research and monitoring. A further advantage is achieved by adopting a broadly focused approach, organising across a range of issues and involving a wide spectrum of constituencies. This keeps gender equity on the front burner.

A potential weakness of this strategy is that officers operating specifically under a "gender equity" banner must carry the flame, so to speak, almost all the time. It is too early to evaluate the long-term success of the process. Time will tell whether the internal driver or champion role can fall away. That will depend on whether everyone on campus will become sufficiently aware of, and concerned about, gender issues to ensure that they are fully integrated into organisational life and culture.

A second lesson can be learnt from the bottom-up approach that was adopted. Conventional wisdom often suggests that the original impetus for organisational change should come from management. In this case the initiative was driven from the bottom, leading to the development and adoption of policies and monitoring mechanisms that affected the entire university. A counter-culture mode was avoided through the active encouragement and support of the rector.

Sceptics may argue that, given the activist culture on campus, top management had little alternative but to attempt to "mainstream" the pressure that was being exerted. Such comment may be valid, but it still does not take away the value derived from harnessing activist energy in a positive manner, rather than ignoring or condemning such efforts.

A final lesson emerges from the link between struggles against racism and sexism. Whilst UWC has always had an active engagement with affirmative action on racial issues, it acknowledged the need to treat gender equity separately rather than under a general rubric of affirmative action. Race and gender issues are closely linked, but they do not emerge from the same set of prejudices. The solution to racial discrimination is therefore not necessarily the solution to gender discrimination. By keeping these issues in close relation to each other, while treating them separately in structural terms, both similarities and differences can be addressed.

REMAINING CHALLENGES

Significant gains have been made in creating an environment where all staff and students can study and work with equal advantage or disadvantage. The gender co-ordinator, however, listed a number of difficulties encountered by the gender equity initiative.

She cited the "culture of entitlement" as one of the main problems. Some black people and women think that society, in this case the university, should compensate them for years of oppression and struggle. The challenge is therefore to make black people and women aware that they should "seize the moment". They should insist on recognition where recognition is due and know how to deliver if they want the appropriate rights and power. Women in particular, she says, should stop playing the "victim" and educate themselves. She points out that there is still not one black woman UWC PhD graduate on campus. This can partly be ascribed to the lack of women academics who can serve as role models to women students, but it is also women's lack of confidence that prevents them from making and taking up opportunities for further study.

She also found that there was a backlash, particularly from black men, against upwardly mobile black and white women. However she cautions women not to identify men as the "enemy", but rather to stop allocating blame and start engaging in constructive ways.

While institutions should provide opportunities for staff development and career building, staff development should also be seen as the individual's responsibility. Seeing staff development as something that the individual does for him/herself does not, however, release faculties and departments from their obligation to take their duties seriously. Many women academics are on contract posts and they do not automatically get sabbatical leave. Heads of departments should fight for study leave for all staff and should actively encourage women to become more assertive and independent.

Gender equity is, therefore, not viewed as incongruent with academic excellence. UWC, like all other tertiary institutions, is feeling the increased pressure to cut costs and still maintain high academic standards. All appointments are carefully considered and candidates are assessed for current and future potential. It is in this context that affirmative action, and gender equity in particular, is pursued. ■

BRITISH PETROLEUM SA

MARE NORVAL

PROFILE OF THE COMPANY

BP International is the third biggest oil company in the world and has approximately 16 to 19 percent of the market share in South Africa. BP Southern Africa (BPSA), a subsidiary of BP (UK), has historically reported directly to London. It also controlled the offices in Lesotho, Botswana and Namibia prior to their independence.

The rest of Africa used to be controlled by BP Africa, which was based in London. However, in 1992, BP Africa moved to Cape Town, using the infrastructure of BPSA, with its chief executive represented on BPSA's executive team.

Staff interviewed at BPSA, including senior managers, agree that the movement towards affirmative action developed as a result of pressure from BP's mother company, BP (UK), to recruit more people of colour.

The distribution of all the staff in the company, as it stood early in 1994, is shown in the table overleaf.

METHOD AND SAMPLE

The interview sample was drawn from BP's head office and from the Cape Town depot staff. The Sapref Refinery in Durban, which is the largest refinery in southern Africa and is jointly owned by BP and Shell, was not included in the survey.

The profile of the work-force is representative of BP offices nationally. A total of 25 interviews were conducted with people selected by the company's affirmative action co-ordinator according to the parameters set out by the researcher. The breakdown of the interview sample is shown on the table on page 109.

■ TABLE 1 ■

PERMANENT STAFF BY RACE, GENDER AND SKILL LEVEL. MARCH 31, 1994

PATERSON GRADE	WHITE	BLACK	COLOURED	ASIAN	TOTAL	WOMEN
NON-EXEC DIRECTORS	0	0	0	0	0	0
F	4	0	0	0	4	0
E 4-5	7	0	1	0	8	0
E 1-3	13	1	0	1	15	0
D 4-5	40	3	1	1	45	3
D 1-3	83	12	7	2	104	8
C 4-5	193	41	56	21	311	60
C 1-3	154	102	114	38	408	110
B	41	278	157	14	490	61
A	0	66	19	0	85	2
TOTAL	535	503	355	77	1470	244

Source: UCT Graduate School of Business — Breakwater Monitor

Notes:

Paterson F	Executive Directors
Paterson E 4-5	Senior — Executive Management
Paterson E 1-3	Senior Management
Paterson D 4-5	Middle — Senior Management
Paterson D 1-3	Junior — Middle Management
Paterson C 4-5	Assistant Management — Senior Supervisory & Junior Professional
Paterson C 1-3	Graduate Entry, Supervisory, Artisan and Technician, Senior Operative and Senior Admin/Clerical/Secretarial
Paterson B	Operative, Admin/Clerical/Secretarial
Paterson A	Entry Level Operative & Labourer

HISTORY OF AFFIRMATIVE ACTION

The organisation started implementing various initiatives from as early as 1977, although a formal policy was only drafted in 1994. While the initiatives will be discussed in chronological order, it should be borne in mind that they proceeded in a somewhat ad hoc manner, rather than as a sequenced pattern of events. Activity has focused mainly on the recruitment and development of black graduates with organisation development and broader staff development emerging as focal points later.

■ TABLE 2 ■

INTERVIEW SAMPLE

	AFRICAN		COLOURED		WHITE		
	M	F	M	F	M	F	Total
SENIOR MANAGEMENT					2		2
MIDDLE/JUNIOR MANAGEMENT	5		5	1	1	1	13
SUPERVISORY/SKILLED		2	1	2	1	4	10
TOTAL	5	2	6	3	4	5	25

PHASE 1: STAFF DEVELOPMENT COMMITTEE 1977–1991

During the early years, progress on affirmative action was slow. Some progress was made in the recruitment of coloured and Asian staff, but not in increasing the number of African staff. Reasons given for this were:
- The Western Cape used to be a coloured labour preference area.
- Whites do not perceive coloureds as alien — as a staff member said: "They are more like whites, the culture is closer, they speak the same language."
- It was difficult to source skilled Africans in Cape Town.
- Organising housing was difficult for Africans if they were not from Cape Town. According to one African man interviewed, he felt isolated in Cape Town and did not like working there for that reason.

The first attempt to formalise responsibility for affirmative action came in 1980 when a human resources staff development committee was formed to initiate, drive and focus on a black advancement programme. This committee consisted of a mix of line managers and human resources staff selected by the chief executive. Each of the initiatives that followed was initiated by this committee.

Recognising their failure to recruit African staff, the first project that this committee launched was the BP Introduction programme (BPI) in 1982. This provided for an intake of African graduates who were separately and intensively trained over a six-month period. They were appointed as "supernumeraries", additional to the normal staff complement. Many of them were never appointed to established posts, though several have apparently done well after taking up appointments in other organisations. One of the few people still working for the company described the programme as "insulting". They were promised positions as managers "in a year's time" which had created unrealistic expectations and disillusionment. This had led to most of the graduates leaving.

The BPI programme in its original form was discontinued after only one intake. An extensively modified version of the programme, however, continued as part of the black graduate programme, whereby black graduates were recruited annually by means of visits to all the major campuses. The company took on about 15 graduates a year of whom 80 percent had BComm degrees and most of the remainder BSc and engineering degrees. Annual graduate recruitment ceased in 1992 as a result of the recession and restructuring in BP and the company now recruits on an ad hoc basis, according to specific requirements. Most graduate recruits already have one or two years' business experience and are expected to make an immediate contribution.

In 1984, the organisation started paying attention to the development of non-graduate staff by means of the Business Development programme. This programme still exists and requires line managers to identify subordinates with potential who will be trained to give them an opportunity to develop and grow in the company. It is a three-week residential programme that covers general induction, product knowledge, interaction, communication and practical business skills.

In 1986, targets were set by the staff development committee in conjunction with line managers. The long-term goal was to match the staff complement at BP to the distribution of the population of the country. Using population projections compiled by the Urban Foundation for the year 2000, the following targets were set:

■ TABLE 3 ■

TARGETS FOR YEAR 2000

	BLACK, COLOURED, ASIAN	WHITE
JOHANNESBURG	78%	22%
DURBAN/EAST LONDON	73%	27%
CAPE TOWN/PORT ELIZABETH	28%	72%
BLOEMFONTEIN	81%	19%

Realising that insufficient Africans were joining the company through the normal recruitment mechanisms, affirmative action practices were reviewed in 1991. This resulted in a decision to confine external recruitment to Africans at entry level and to target high potential Africans for appointment to certain senior, supervisory and management level positions.

In order to achieve these targets, a set of programmes was introduced. A Career Development programme was initiated in 1991, aimed at advancing graduates into management positions within five years. The programme included the following activities:

- Outward bound courses.
- A professional BP-specific assessment.
- A career development workshop exploring the development process in the context of South Africa and BPSA.
- The formulation of a realistic development plan.

Candidates with potential for the Career Development programme were identified by line managers for assessment of their managerial potential. The process involved evaluation on six dimensions and was carried out by external consultants. Career path appreciation and a one-day assessment were investigated in 1991 for the recruitment of graduates but these were never used as new graduates were not entering the organisation. A basic needs assessment for all staff was also undertaken in the same year, and formulated into a personal development plan. For the first time, the scope of development activities was broadened to include all staff and not only targeted groupings.

At the same time a value sharing project, called Leadership in Change (Linc), was launched as it was recognised that there were no easy ways of changing the way people thought and acted. The entire staff had to be taken through a programme that would enable them not only to understand what was happening, but also why the company was changing. The introductory stage therefore consisted of a series of workshops that covered five core elements:

- The vision of BPSA as a successful oil company.
- The essential Linc behaviours (how employees should conduct themselves in the work-place) which included openness, personal impact, empowerment and networking.
- Values – what is important to the company and what will drive BPSA in the future.
- Strategy – where the company was going and why.
- Action plans – employees had to develop plans of how they, as individuals and as part of a team, would contribute to the process of change.

Between April 1991 and May 1992, every BPSA employee attended a Linc workshop. Problems such as management style, communication, training, rewards and staff development were freely and openly discussed. According to staff interviewed, senior managers provided answers to delegates' queries in an open and honest way.

PHASE 2: 1992 ONWARDS

BPSA started down-sizing in 1990 in preparation for the deregulation that all petrol companies were anticipating. This resulted in steady retrenchments and no further recruitment of new staff. In terms of affirmative action, the effect of restructuring was felt not so much through the number of black staff who were retrenched. Rather, the company was unable to continue its external recruitment of black staff at entry level or targeting blacks for appointment to senior level positions.

Within the context of restructuring, responsibility for black advancement changed hands. In 1992, business managers with line responsibility were allocated the affirmative action function, which had previously resided with the staff development committee. This was changed in order to drive the affirmative action initiative from the top down. Human resources personnel were expected to help and advise business managers.

The business managers abandoned the 1986 targets because they believed that they were unrealistic, especially with respect to Africans. They believed that the programme had become a numbers game and, rather than targets, they would prefer to have different pressures placed on them. The following monitoring categories were introduced in 1993:

- A comparison of the numbers and percentages of black, coloured and white staff for junior management and above.
- The progress of black staff in job grades.
- The perceived leadership on the issue (ie the number of occasions the subject is raised in public meetings, management meetings, etc).
- The existence of a longer term manpower plan/analysis.
- The existence of longer term career plans for black staff.
- The extent to which black staff are made available for other departments.
- The number of black staff recruited.
- The number of black staff who resigned.
- The extent to which a black advancement budget was used.
- The number of personal development programmes/appraisals done.
- The extent to which planned training was realised.
- The status of a mentoring programme.
- The extent to which potential performance problems were identified/solved.
- Progress made on following-up "Understanding Racism" workshops.
- The plans/commitment to have black staff directly reporting to managers/ department heads.
- The acceptance by black staff of the programme/policy.

The first evaluation of these monitoring mechanisms was in progress at the time of compiling this case study.

As staff development features prominently in the new guidelines, a mentoring system was introduced in 1993 with a designated post of a mentoring co-ordinator created in the human resources department. The plan is that new black staff, both those with experience and new graduates, will be linked to a senior person in BPSA. Ideally this person will not be from the new recruit's immediate area.

Broader organisation development work continued through a further sharing initiative, "Understanding Racism" workshops, introduced in 1993 to address attitudes to race and gender issues. The exercises, videos and discussions are held in facilitated, interactive groups. The workshop groups are mixed in gender, race and status levels to break down stereotyped thinking and misconceptions. Workshops are run by outside consultants who train staff within BPSA to run groups throughout the company. The favourable response to these workshops has led BPSA to explore running related workshops to ensure ongoing change.

EVALUATION OF THE POLICY

It is evident that BPSA has focused mainly on three processes: graduate intake, internal staff development and organisational development. During interviews with staff a number of problems were raised with these activities.

COMMUNICATION

There appears to be a lack of communication with staff about the affirmative action initiative at BPSA. The majority of black and lower level white staff know very little about the objectives and goals. Senior staff, white staff and human resources staff who were interviewed thought that it was little more than an image-building exercise for the company to present itself favourably in the business environment. Attempts to improve communication through the value-sharing workshops have, however, been well received.

BENEFICIARIES

Because its head office is in the Western Cape, BPSA raises the question of how one deals with the issue of coloureds being the majority of black people in this region. A coloured employee puts the question starkly: "I am also black. Why don't I excel as quickly as my black (African) counterparts?"

Some employees felt that Africans would have viewed the various programmes more positively if there had been an African on the staff development committee and in the business managers' unit. An African support or interest group would also have helped. As one senior African interviewee asked: "How can they (coloureds and whites) decide who we are and how we should move forward?"

It appears that, over the last couple of years, more Africans have been promoted than coloured staff. Coloured staff interviewed said they had never felt part of a programme that was supposed to have been to their advantage. In the early years of BPSA's affirmative action initiative, there was no urgency to develop coloured people at the same pace as Africans. One coloured middle manager said ironically: "First we were not white enough, now we are not black enough".

RECRUITMENT AND SELECTION

Some interviewees felt that the abolition of annual graduate recruitment was short-sighted as it would create a lack of junior managers in the next few years. In their view, BPSA should continue to invest in the recruitment and training of graduates on a planned basis. Interviewees also felt that prospective employees were not properly assessed in terms of potential and that overqualified and often underqualified staff were recruited, resulting in boredom or demotivation.

MENTORING

Interviewees had mixed feelings about the mentoring or "buddying" supervisory system. Some considered mentoring to be artificial. Some black employees felt that whites had exclusive networks in the company because they had universities, schools, clubs and residential areas in common. This resulted in blacks being unable to link up with influential white staff. Some senior white managers described mentoring as counter-productive. One said: "It becomes a protective umbrella". They believed that, should blacks overcome the obstacles on their own, they would emerge stronger and wiser.

Some, however, saw prospects for promotion improving as a result of a successful mentoring process which made blacks more visible. Black staff also felt there was room for a reverse mentoring situation with whites learning more from black culture.

PROMOTIONS

According to one of the business managers, the biggest stumbling block was the development of staff from the supervisor and middle management levels to senior management levels and above. He said the main difficulty was having to displace the excellent whites already in those grades in order to make room for blacks. He added that at each monthly career development meeting where the promotion prospects of blacks at these levels were discussed the conclusion was "he/she is very good but not ready yet".

Business managers believed that top management was sincere about change and that there was no deliberate blocking of blacks as some black staff members suggested. They acknowledged, however, that the company's perceived model of success was a white, Eurocentric one.

Many of the black staff interviewed felt, however, that development and growth in their jobs had not materialised. They believed that real change would only come about with a shift of control to black people. They said it was only a matter of time before a senior black executive, who had been with the company for a long time, became chairman. One or two other black individuals were mentioned as having moved sideways and then advancing substantially after that.

In these cases there had been a successful match between skills and job requirements. Several suggestions were made by senior managers about how to develop black staff to senior management and above. They said this could include an exchange programme to other BPSA offices, particularly in Africa, as these were generally smaller. This would give exchange candidates greater access and broader experience. The company is examining the possibility of sending staff on a six month to one year on-the-job training programme. This would be cheaper and less threatening to whites as it would be seen as part of training rather than taking over someone else's job.

In our interviews with depot staff it became clear that many people felt isolated and uninformed about the process of change. They felt that if a Chemical Workers' Industrial Union representative was included in the affirmative action structures, progress could be made in training and this would improve the prospects of depot staff being promoted to head office.

GENDER ISSUES

Women felt that they were unrepresented and ignored. From the earliest affirmative action programme, no mention has been made of gender inequalities. Executive managers agreed that this matter needed serious attention, but no plans have been made in this regard.

CONCLUSION

BPSA was one of the first South African companies to embark on what was then called black advancement. It was a problematic route from the beginning for two reasons. Firstly, at the time there were very few positive role models of successful programmes. Secondly, their head office was situated in a predominantly coloured area and special programmes for African graduates were not seen to be addressing the development needs and aspirations of a large portion of the work-force.

It is clear that BPSA has invested resources in setting up a range of special programmes. The process by which these programmes were identified, however, appears to have been ad hoc. One of the underlying reasons for this may have been the absence, until recently, of a clearly formulated policy. Even though targets were set, they were not systematically monitored and evaluated and a basis for future planning was, therefore, not established.

Much has been done to promote career development for all staff. Many of these programmes, such as the personal development plan, focus on individual needs and requirements. Organisational barriers to development should form the next focal area.

The distinction between coloureds and Africans emerged as a crucial issue in the case study. A lesson to be learned from this is that organisations need to debate the question of beneficiaries, involve staff in the discussion and make explicit the rationale for the final decision. It is also clear that the development of women will not occur without the organisation taking a clear stance.

A final lesson is that the implementation of separate programmes for black staff often leads to dissatisfaction both for those on the programmes and for those excluded. The appointment of affirmative action employees to supernumerate positions increases the difficulty of integration.

BPSA is to be commended for its early initiatives at a time when affirmative action was not as well publicised and researched as it is now. The case study illustrates the rich variety of programmes that can promote affirmative action, but also cautions against some of the pitfalls that should be avoided by organisations embarking on this route. ■

PICK 'N PAY

PROFILE OF THE COMPANY

At 1am one morning in 1967, a deal was struck that enabled Raymond
Ackerman to acquire four small supermarkets in Cape Town. This heralded the
beginning of the Pick 'n Pay group. Twenty-six years later the store count
stands at 107 supermarkets, 14 hypermarkets, 11 Boardmans, eight Price
Clubs and three Chain Reaction stores.

The organisation's mission statement reads as follows: "Our aim is to
distribute manufactured goods and agricultural products efficiently and to
interpret and satisfy consumer demand."

Building on its small beginnings in Cape Town, the engine room of the Pick
'n Pay retail empire has remained in Cape Town. This case study focuses on
Pick 'n Pay in the Western Cape, its supermarkets and hypermarkets.

Food retailing, in the form of supermarkets, came to South Africa in the
early 1950s. Monumental changes have occurred since then in the growth of
supermarket chains, superstores and hypermarkets. An interviewee (manager)
believes that Pick 'n Pay has been able to survive these changes because the
company was able to adapt to different markets in the retail sector. The
company also had the foresight to invest in technology. Its financial structuring
and its stoic adherence to its core business focus, retailing, has ensured that
today Pick 'n Pay's market share is one-third of the retail sector.

In 1984, Pick 'n Pay diversified from mass retailing by acquiring a 50
percent interest in the homewares division, Boardmans. In 1986, an
experiment with wholesaling under the Price Club banner revealed that the
cash and carry concept provided considerable business potential, particularly
given the growing entrepreneurial spirit among black traders in South Africa.
The latest diversification of the group is into Chain Reaction which serves the
speciality clothing market. Pick 'n Pay is now hoping to tap into the low-
income market through the acquisition of the Score supermarket chain.

Pick 'n Pay is a family business. It is controlled by Ackerman, who is the

— 117 —

chairperson. His wife is a director, while their elder son is joint managing director and managing director of the Blue Ribbon meat corporation. According to Ackerman:

> Since we all share great conviction in the future of South Africa and the success of Pick 'n Pay, we are unanimous in our view both to remain fully involved in the future management of Pick 'n Pay and to retain the controlling interest in the group[1].

To ensure the family's control of the company, a holding company, Pick 'n Pay Holdings (Pikwik), was established to retain control of at least 50 percent of Pick 'n Pay while the Ackerman family retains control of Pikwik. In addition, a chairperson's committee, with Raymond Ackerman as its chairperson, has been established to identify and initiate matters of major strategy and policy.

Managers interviewed believed that the corporation had been able to remain a market leader in the sector because of its philosophy of "consumer sovereignty," described by Raymond Ackerman as: "If we (Pick 'n Pay) make the consumers feel like queens and if we act as if the consumer is queen, she or he would make us the king." Ackerman sees the consumer sitting on a table which is supported by four legs – merchandising, people, administration and sales promotion. He believes that the art of retailing lies in successfully balancing these four legs.

Pick 'n Pay's success has not gone unchallenged: not only has it been pressurised by the competition in the retail sector, but the organisation has also been challenged by workers on the shop floor. Those managers interviewed did not hesitate to acknowledge that the unionisation of its weekly paid staff by the South African Commercial, Catering and Allied Workers Union has had a major impact on the company's culture and industrial relations policy. (The company experienced a punishing strike soon after the researcher had conducted interviews with staff.) Management now recognises the need for collective bargaining and willingness to bargain has resulted in the company having one of the most comprehensive maternity benefit packages in the industry.

Pick 'n Pay operates on a policy of decentralisation. Each store and hypermarket operates as an independent cost centre. This is supported by a decentralised management policy. There are 22 separate operating units plus the corporate unit. Each does its own buying, accounting, warehousing, etc. According to the chairperson, "each general manager is an entrepreneur with bottom-line responsibility, though I have an overall guiding hand" (*Annual Report*, 1993).

A handful of top executives exercise group responsibility for each discipline – finance, promotion, personnel, etc – and liaise with regional

---

1. *Ackerman, R. 1982.* The Pick 'n Pay Story. *Internal Document.*

managers to control policy directives. Regional managements have freedom to make all decisions except those concerning capital investments and site location.

Rapid population growth and urbanisation have resulted in the expansion of the low-income market and Pick 'n Pay recognises that this is where much of its future growth will lie. Further opportunities for expansion, both retail and wholesale, await in southern and central Africa. Namibia and Botswana are likely starting points, and it is in this context that the pressures for affirmative action are most visible.

By October 1993, Pick 'n Pay had a national staff complement of 28 790, excluding main board members. The geographical distribution of Pick 'n Pay employees was as follows: Western Cape 6 066; Eastern Cape 2 277; Natal 4 161; Orange Free State 1 964; Southern Transvaal 10 810; and Northern Transvaal 3 163.

The majority of employees (47 percent) are weekly-paid full-time employees and 33 percent are weekly-paid casual or part time employees. In other words, 80 percent of Pick 'n Pay employees are paid weekly.

The racial and gender composition of the organisation's permanent staff, in March 1994, is shown in the table overleaf:

METHOD AND SAMPLE

Between March and May 1994, 32 interviews were conducted, as shown in the table below. They were selected to get the views of a cross-section of staff and were identified by a contact person in the human resources department. Only people at the head office and at Cape Town stores were interviewed.

■ TABLE 1 ■

	MEN				WOMEN				
	AS	A	C	W	AS	A	C	W	Total
GEN MANAGER			1	3					4
SEN MAN				3				1	4
STORE MAN		1	1	1		1		2	6
FLOOR MAN	2	1	1						4
TRAINEE							1		1
SUPERVISOR		1	2				2		5
WEEKLY PAID		1	3			1	3		8
TOTAL	2	4	8	7		2	6	3	32

■ TABLE 2 ■

PERMANENT STAFF STRENGTH BY RACE, GENDER AND SKILL LEVEL, MARCH 31, 1994

PATERSON	WHITE	AFRICAN	COLOURED	ASIAN	TOTAL	WOMEN
NON-EXEC DIRECTORS	4	0	0	0	4	0
F	10	0	0	0	10	1
E 4-5	67	0	1	3	71	2
E 1-3	159	3	8	5	175	12
D 4-5						
D 1-3	272	15	38	23	348	0
C 1-5	2 160	1 221	1 437	344	5 162	2 387
B - A	512	9 522	3 432	668	14 134	8 222
TOTAL	3 184	10 761	4 916	1 043	19 904	10 682

Source: UCT Graduate School of Business — Breakwater Monitor

Notes:

Paterson F	Executive Directors
Paterson E 4-5	Senior — Executive Management
Paterson E 1-3	Senior Management
Paterson D 4-5	Middle — Senior Management
Paterson D 1-3	Junior — Middle Management
Paterson C 4-5	Assistant Management, Senior Supervisory and Junior Professional
Paterson C 1-3	Graduate entry, Supervisory, Artisan and Technician, Senior Operative and Senior Admin/Clerical/Secretarial
Paterson B	Operative/Admin/Clerical/Secretarial
Paterson A	Entry Level Operative and Labourer.

HISTORY OF AFFIRMATIVE ACTION

The management interviewed at Pick 'n Pay insisted that it had always been an equal opportunity company. It was said that the chairperson had a "passion" for equal opportunity. Staff agreed that they had always been told that Pick 'n Pay was an equal opportunity company.

In April 1992, an African Managers' Conference was held to discuss how African managers felt about the company and how they were affected by the company's policies. The major point of discussion at the conference was black advancement at Pick 'n Pay. It was the first time that this issue was openly discussed in the organisation.

After the conference, a committee was established, consisting of members who had attended the conference, to discuss black advancement with their respective regional managers. Members were also asked to review and offer suggestions about a document, drawn up by the main board of Pick 'n Pay, called *Affirmative Action Project 1992 - 2000*. This document contained an action plan for the implementation of affirmative action in each region.

The document provided details of the following:
- Training and recruitment by region, for example the number of people to receive training, sources for recruitment and estimated cost of payroll.
- Training courses deemed necessary for affirmative action plans to succeed.
- Identifying black employees for advancement in each region.
- Targets for management level positions for each region by 2000.

AFFIRMATIVE ACTION PROJECT 1992-2000

At Pick 'n Pay, affirmative action is seen as an integral part of personnel planning. The document gives the following reasons for implementing affirmative action:

> Skills shortages – By the year 2000 South Africa will be suffering gross management shortages. Pick 'n Pay will be similarly affected unless we do something about it now. This has nothing to do with race – it is a business imperative.

> We must practise affirmative action for economic reasons – unless all human potential is identified and developed in our company, we cannot enjoy the full benefit of this area of contribution.

> A new political dispensation may expect managerial structures to reflect the community at large. Unless we become pro-active and pre-empt this situation, we may be forced to comply with imposed targets which may mean the spectre of tokenism.

For Pick 'n Pay, affirmative action means the same as black advancement and equal opportunity, but it prefers the term affirmative action because it "implies a positive and conscious intervention".

This document laid the basis of Pick 'n Pay's affirmative action programme. The programme was circulated to all managers and was accompanied by another document explaining why the company was adopting it, describing who was to benefit, outlining goals and allocating responsibility for monitoring. The document also described how affirmative action should be communicated through the organisation, how potential for the affirmative action programme should be identified and how training and development would be provided.

It was decided to appoint an affirmative action "champion" to drive the policy within the organisation and the human resources general manager was chosen. Discussion below will reveal that the appointment of a champion is a potentially sensitive issue. Regions and stores were asked to appoint affirmative action champions who would be responsible for implementing the programme at shop floor level.

TRAINING AND DEVELOPMENT

> The paradigm driving any affirmative action programme must be embedded in the desire to train and develop people for their own sake and for the sake of enhancing their productivity and worth to the organisation. When we do identify people for affirmative action ... we check what they know and supply them with what they need to know against measurable job requirements.

This encapsulates Pick 'n Pay's approach to training and development. It is specified in the *Affirmative Action Manager's Guide*, which accompanied the *Affirmative Action Project 1992-2000* document.

The management of Pick 'n Pay identified training courses for each store and hypermarket to support the affirmative action programme. These courses ranged from advanced finance budgeting and management skills and principles, to report writing and life skills. It also introduced a model for employee development that included a range of training and development activities. "Graduates" from these courses were given company certificates.

Pick 'n Pay also introduced an affirmative action bridging programme. Its aim was to provide opportunities to develop staff members who had the potential to become managers but who did not yet have the required qualifications and skills.

Candidates had to apply for admission and were selected through interviews. They were rated according to their ability and willingness to further themselves. Selection for the programme was, however, not to be viewed as promotion. The company made it clear that the only benefit to the individual would be the opportunity to learn and develop skills. The programme covered literacy and numeracy training, supervisory skills, computer literacy and basic business principles.

The implementation of affirmative action at management level was through what Pick 'n Pay called a "mini MBA". To meet the future demand for managers, Pick 'n Pay placed a few African managers on a three-year study programme. The aim was to have 12 trainee managers in every three-year cycle.

The management responsible for drawing up the affirmative action policy document also believed that it was important to set affirmative action goals. The reasons were:
- To have goals against which development plans can be measured.
- To actively identify potential staff for training and development.
- To determine acceptable and meaningful levels of "racial" mix in management structures.

GOALS

The management of the individual stores and hypermarkets recommended specific goals for their stores and these were translated into targets. The targets were detailed in *Affirmative Action Project 1992-2000*.

RESPONSIBILITY

The management team that formulated the policy document believed that affirmative action, like all management development activity, had to be the function and responsibility of the line management. However, each store was also asked to appoint an affirmative action champion to drive the initiative at the shop floor level while the personnel planning general manager was responsible for the overall programme.

The regional/chief and general managers monitored affirmative action and it was also their task to strategise and create opportunities and a culture that would ensure that affirmative action took place. The human resource division in the region played a strong monitoring and advisory role and assisted with implementation.

Key to Pick 'n Pay's operational strategy is the policy of decentralisation. Affirmative action strategies, like all others, are driven regionally. The regions are seen to be responsible for the following:
- Setting, implementing and controlling their own affirmative action strategies.
- Conducting their own needs analysis to determine and develop affirmative action strategies.

Pick 'n Pay management sees itself as encouraging the implementation of affirmative action by:
- Including affirmative action as a key result area in the performance appraisal system.
- Including affirmative action in the company's remuneration criteria.
- Getting feedback from the affirmative action office to the main board twice a year on the achievement of affirmative action goals.

LATEST DEVELOPMENTS

By the end of 1993, very little progress had been made in implementing affirmative action. A member of the committee elected at the African Managers' Conference said:

> The document lay in the safe for a year, members of the committee became
> disillusioned, we had a plan but no authority to implement. If your general
> manager did not support the initiative then there was nothing that could be
> done.

At the end of 1993, the document was revisited and an affirmative action committee meeting was scheduled for March 1994 to revive the initiative.

In April 1994, economic conditions had forced Pick 'n Pay to reconsider its staff complement. In an effort to reduce numbers, an early retirement package was offered to staff. The company's affirmative action champion accepted the offer and retired. By May 1994, the manpower planning general manager had taken over the affirmative action portfolio.

He decided that the programme would be more effective if it was implemented by a committee rather than an individual. The new committee consists of individuals who work in areas believed to be relevant to affirmative action: marketing and communication, testing and recruitment, training, manpower planning and industrial relations. It is envisaged that this committee will provide advice, guidance and benchmarking in the areas in which they have expertise. Affirmative action will continue to be driven from the local level, with each store and hypermarket having its own programme.

Each region and hypermarket has had to complete a questionnaire on progress made to date on affirmative action, based on the targets that were set for each region and hypermarket in *Affirmative Action Project 1992-2000*. At the time of this research the committee was due to meet to discuss the results of the questionnaire, after which appropriate follow-up action was to be planned.

So much depends on the person who is appointed the store champion that Pick 'n Pay might have to reconsider the selection of these champions. The company did not specify selection criteria when it started the initiative and staff have already questioned some of the selections.

EVALUATION OF THE POLICY

LACK OF CLARITY ON BENEFICIARIES

Management has defined beneficiaries as all employees with special needs: blacks (ie coloureds, Asians, Africans) and women. Interviews revealed that opinions among staff differed as to who affirmative action should target. A few believed that the country's demography should determine the target constituency while others believed that affirmative action should be applied fairly to every person who had been disadvantaged. Some believed affirmative action should be for Africans only, while others believed Africans were not the only ones who were disadvantaged by apartheid. A few supported the notion of "disadvantaged by degree" and said that benefits should accrue by degree. Others said that, in terms of real power and authority, all blacks were disadvantaged equally.

In the Western Cape, coloureds makes up the largest proportion of the population. Management believed that it had already succeeded in affirming coloured employees. The table overleaf demonstrates, however, that few

TABLE 3

DISTRIBUTION OF MANAGERS
IN THE WESTERN CAPE

CATEGORY	ASIAN	AFRICAN	COLOURED	WHITE	TOTAL
MAIN BOARD	0	0	0	0	0
LOCAL BOARD	0	0	0	6	6
SENIOR MANAGER	0	0	1	15 (1)	16
MANAGER	1	0	15 (1)	21	37
ASSISTANT MAN		2 (1)	37 (3)	52 (16)	91
FLOOR MANAGER		2	56 (9)	22 (15)	80
TOTAL	1	4	109	116	230
( ) = WOMEN					

coloureds have been able to rise through the ranks. It also confirms that black people are not well represented at senior management level.

In the context of the Western Cape, management has not been able to resolve the dilemma of what constitutes a representative work-force. No affirmative action legislation exists to help the company make this decision. Management has been reluctant to take a position that might come into conflict with future legislation. One of the opinions expressed was:

> We are not in a black community, we're in a coloured community, and that is the composition of our staff. We'll be false if we suddenly employ more Africans.

COMMUNICATION

At Pick 'n Pay, the initial drive for an affirmative action policy came from the chairperson. Unfortunately this top down approach was not successful in communicating the policy to the rest of the organisation. Interviews revealed that even among management, there were those who were not aware of Pick 'n Pay's affirmative action programme. This included the majority of employees on the shop floor. According to one senior manager interviewed, "if Pick 'n Pay has an affirmative action programme then they have not made it known".

Some managers knew about the programme, but this knowledge was sometimes accompanied by uncertainty, especially among white managers:

> Affirmative action must not become reverse discrimination ... Affirmative action means that there is favouritism instead of fairness. (Interview with white manager.)

Other comments include:

> The union knows nothing about Pick 'n Pay having an affirmative action
> programme. The people on the shop floor do not know about it. (Interview with
> shop steward.)

> I haven't heard that Pick 'n Pay has an affirmative action programme. (Interview
> with a weekly paid worker.)

These were common responses from people interviewed, many of whom
were also not clear what affirmative action was all about. This lack of
communication to people on the shop floor gave rise to tensions and fears
amongst coloured people, who said:

> If Africans take over, what's going to happen to the coloureds? Apartheid
> between black and white will be dead, but between blacks there will be
> apartheid.

> The blacks don't like us, they will oppress us when they take over.

The uncertainty and fear that surrounds the issue of affirmative action may
also account for the lack of progress made in implementing the programme.

IMPLEMENTATION

After the African Managers' Conference in 1992, the human resources general
manager, who was black, was appointed to drive the affirmative action
programme. Interviews reveal that some managers questioned how serious Pick
'n Pay was in implementing the programme as they did not think that the
human resources manager had enough authority vis-à-vis the other
management portfolios. Some thought that making a black person responsible
for the affirmative action programme would compromise the individual.

By the start of 1994, the implementation of the programme had not got off
the ground. The reasons for this were not clear but interviews reveal that
issues such as the lack of communication and commitment to the programme
were possible explanations. The following are some of the comments made by
employees:

> I know they (Pick 'n Pay) have an affirmative action programme. I heard them
> talking, but I don't know how they're implementing it. I haven't seen any
> changes yet.

> I believe our general manager is committed to change but I am not so sure about
> his managers. They agree to things when the general manager is present but I
> don't think they believe in it.

A further obstacle to the implementation of the project was that the priority of the project was not clearly defined. While the programme document specified the period 1992-2000, no guidelines and specific monitoring mechanisms were included. It was also felt that although Pick 'n Pay had always had an equal opportunity policy, some managers believed that this was about getting the numbers right. Others believed that it was about people development and a belief in people's abilities.

In addition, some said that the ethos of the company was subconsciously racist. They said a stereotype existed that in order to be successful in retailing you had to be white and male. Thus, the stereotype continues, women are only interested in "soft jobs", while blacks simply cannot cope with the rigours of this sector.

RECRUITMENT

Explanations differed as to why Pick 'n Pay had not been successful in recruiting or developing African staff. Some managers acknowledged that Pick 'n Pay had not been active enough, or that Africans were perceived by some management as not being able to cope with the rigorous pace of the retail sector. Others believed Africans had not been sufficiently patient. Africans were also perceived to prefer less stressful occupations. It was felt that the long hours and low wages did not appeal to them, especially in view of the lucrative offers to them from other organisations.

Women make up a large proportion of Pick 'n Pay's work-force. However, as in most companies, they mainly occupy the lower levels in the organisation. This is not likely to change in the near future since managers admit that they do not have enough women trainees in the system. This is largely the result of the stereotyped attitudes of male managers who believe that retailing is a man's job; that, along with blacks, women just do not have what it takes to be successful. Further probing on this issue of "what it takes" did not reveal much more than the fact that women would not, for example, be willing to go to the store in the middle of the night when the alarm went off. This is a very real danger, but according to some of the managers interviewed, these problems are not insurmountable.

RESTRUCTURING

Adverse economic conditions have resulted in many companies finding themselves overstaffed. Pick 'n Pay is no exception. In response to a question about how the company would implement affirmative action given the current freeze on recruitment from outside, some managers said that affirmative action could be accommodated in a recessionary climate. While it could not be implemented on the desired scale, the recession did not prevent management from identifying staff with potential, identifying their needs and providing them with the necessary skills training. In fact, the freeze on recruitment forced management to look harder for potential inside the company.

The reality at Pick 'n Pay has, however, been slightly different. Some managers interviewed believed that the company did not have enough blacks within the organisation who could be groomed for management positions. This had forced the company to look outside. Others admitted that because the company had not been active enough in identifying and developing black staff, the short-term solution was to make a few external appointments. To put this into effect, an outside consultant was hired to find black trainees.

TRAINING

Pick 'n Pay store managers are responsible for identifying people with potential. The *Affirmative Action Managers' Guide* explains how this should be done but the managers admitted that their selection was purely subjective. Implementing affirmative action is hindered by the unwillingness of some managers to groom trainees because they see them as threats to their own jobs. Trainees who were interviewed felt that the goal posts were being shifted and that they were being kept at trainee status for longer than necessary. They believed that opportunities were more quickly identified for white trainees than for blacks:

> Whites don't have to go through the ranks as coloureds have to. Whites come in as management trainees.

A few comments on how employees feel about affirmative action:

> I see myself as a token, I hate it.

> Blacks are getting the positions but not the benefits that go with it, eg equal remuneration.

> You might be an affirmative action candidate but you already possess the qualifications. Colleagues need to be made aware of this.

CONCLUSION

Pick 'n Pay has always viewed itself as an equal opportunity company. Changes in the political environment have encouraged black employees to raise the specific issue of the advancement of blacks within the organisation. Black employees interviewed felt that even though Pick 'n Pay has an equal opportunity policy, they had not progressed as far and as fast as white employees had. They, therefore, believed that specific action was needed to address the advancement of blacks in the organisation.

Even though the African Managers' Conference had been held in April

1992, little progress had been made by the end of 1993 in implementing the programme. The lack of communication of the policy, the unwillingness of line managers to train and identify affirmative action candidates and the selection of inappropriate champions were all cited as possible reasons.

By May 1994, the management of the company decided to review the issue of affirmative action. Affirmative action was seen as an integral part of manpower planning but management was aware that the new government could pass legislation forcing them to implement an affirmative action programme that was not "beneficial" to the company.

Although the company had always prided itself on having equal opportunity policies, this in itself has not been enough to ensure that its management structure represented the broader population.

Although coloureds managed to move through the ranks, they were not able to progress as fast as their white colleagues. Conscious intervention is thus necessary. Even though Pick 'n Pay had drawn up an affirmative action strategy that was supported by the chairperson, the implementation of the programme almost came to a complete standstill. This is not surprising since the majority of employees did not even know that the company had an affirmative action programme.

There are a number of reasons for this. While the company made provision in its budget to implement the programme, the commitment to implement it was absent. The appointment of sometimes inappropriate champions was a further obstacle because employees felt that this was an indication of management's lack of commitment to affirmative action.

The issue of training also holds a lesson. Various training opportunities were identified which the management of the company felt would help the development of affirmative action employees. While these courses were successful at management level, lower level employees did not see their value as they were not related to remuneration. There is also the perception among some black trainees that they are being trained for too long.

Pick 'n Pay is a dynamic company and is at the forefront of many innovative developments in the retail sector. Some know it as a caring company. This is demonstrated by its willingness to address the issue of affirmative action. As the managers now know, however, intention alone does not guarantee success. While the chairperson supported the initiative, procedures were not in place to ensure that those responsible for implementing the programme shared his vision. ■

PART TWO

LESSONS LEARNED

CHAPTER 3

RE-THINKING AFFIRMATIVE ACTION IN THE LIGHT OF THE CASE STUDIES

WHAT THE CASE STUDIES TELL US

The case studies give us a very useful "inside" view of the wide range of initiatives embarked upon under the banner of affirmative action. Each organisation has its own history, traditions, values, driving forces and resource bases. Each uses its resources in particular ways and encounters particular obstacles and difficulties. While it is not appropriate to regard any of the case studies as positive or negative role models, recurrent themes or trends do emerge.

We will briefly identify some of the trends that can be drawn from the case studies as general conclusions and analyse their underlying assumptions and problems in greater depth. Our observations are not offered in any particular order, nor do we attempt to make value judgements about the activities of the organisations that participated in the study. It is, however, important to build a basis for analysis and reflection that will help newcomers to affirmative action. At the same time, those that have already initiated affirmative action strategies will be able to consider their own activities within a wider framework.

COMMON TRENDS

Empirical evidence in the case studies substantiates the following general conclusions:

1. The idea that most affirmative action initiatives are driven by a well-intentioned but naive "bleeding heart brigade" is not confirmed by the case studies. The decision to embark on an affirmative action route was, in all instances, a strategic decision prompted by different combinations of external and internal forces.

    ### EXTERNAL:

    - The changing political scenario and possibilities for economic growth and international trade.
    - Company ownership changes and, for parastatals, a change in government.
    - A surge in demands for equality by the people of South Africa.
    - The need for organisations to achieve congruence between their employee composition and their client or market base in terms of race, gender and language.
    - Pressure exerted by parent companies susceptible to international and local perceptions and opinions.
    - Anticipation of affirmative action legislation that will lay down criteria and introduce penalties for non-compliance.

INTERNAL:

- Demands by employee organisations and trade unions for the training, development and advancement of their members.
- Pressure from informal and formal lobby groups around gender equality and black advancement.
- Pressure from human resource departments for more progressive human resource development practices, including affirmative action.

2. The commitment and contribution of the chief executive emerged as a vital factor. The enthusiastic and dedicated efforts of individuals and affirmative action committees or groupings failed if their endeavours were not actively endorsed and supported by the chief executive.

3. Some organisations embarked upon affirmative action in a planned and systematic way and developed policies that could be monitored and reviewed. Others proceeded in an ad hoc manner that led to a stop-go pattern, limited internal coherence and no basis for systematic evaluation. Even when affirmative action was stated as a strategic imperative, it was not always treated in the same way as, or linked to, other strategic issues. It was also not conceptualised, planned, implemented, reviewed and evaluated in the same way.

4. While most organisations initially concentrated on widening their recruitment base, the emphasis is increasingly shifting to a concern about the retention and development of staff.

5. Many organisations are still battling to make a decision about the appropriate beneficiaries of affirmative action. While black people are the prime target, the term "black" has different meanings. Sometimes it means African people only, at other times it includes coloured and Asian people. "Equity" issues that are receiving attention in a number of other countries are seldom addressed. These include the development and advancement of women, removal of prejudice against gays and lesbians, provision for the disabled to take up their positions as economically active citizens and a more equitable distribution of resources between urban and rural areas.

6. Where targets have been set, they have mostly been general and non-specific. Targets are often not differentiated by occupation or job grade or level. Organisations could therefore achieve general percentage increases without having to consider the over- or under-representation of the groupings targeted for affirmative action. Indicators of "systemic discrimination" (see Chapter 1) are therefore obscured. Where targets do exist, mechanisms for meeting them are often not introduced.

7. Many organisations initially recruited qualified black people and women from outside, often paying high premiums, rather than investing in internal staff development. While there is a shift towards trying to achieve a balance between internal and external recruitment and promotion, the issue remains problematic and contributes to resentment and disillusionment by long-serving employees. Internal barriers to advancement emerged in almost every instance. They include the following:

   • A barrier at a certain point in the organisational hierarchy when a degree or a professional qualification becomes a prerequisite. Employees who have gained competence and experience through internal staff development often "plateau" at this level and do not advance to higher levels. High-level positions are filled by bringing people in from outside who are deemed to have the required skills profile.

   • An almost impenetrable barrier between salaried and weekly-paid staff. The latter category normally consists of the so-called semi-skilled and unskilled employees. Organisations often set affirmative action targets only for management or for salaried staff. This is to the detriment of the people who have historically been most disadvantaged, have very little bargaining power in the labour market and are consequently easily expendable.

   • In some organisations advancement tracks are seen as specialised routes. Lack of job sharing, job rotation or job enrichment opportunities prevent those who are not in a particular job track from gaining the skills and experience that may make them eligible for advancement. Departments or work units are often seen as so different from one another that similarities between the competencies required are obscured. Horizontal progression is not considered as an option when it means transferring across these barriers.

   • Certain occupations or job categories at managerial, supervisory and shop-floor level are still reserved for men only – not as policy, but by common consent. This makes it very difficult for women to gain entry to such positions.

8. Lack of internal discussion and debate about the aims and purposes of affirmative action emerged as one of the most common criticisms. Another was the lack of representative organisational participation in policy development and implementation.

9. Lack of top-to-bottom communication when a strategy or policy had been formulated was another weakness. Despite briefing sessions and video presentations, the message seemed to get stuck somewhere along the line – leading to complaints from staff that they do not know what is going on.

10. Except in some instances, little formal attention has been paid to the transformation of organisational culture. Some organisations have invested in, for example, anti-racism or anti-sexism workshops, diversity games and value-sharing sessions. But cultures tend to be seen as something that concerns only the individual or group and not as an issue that needs to be addressed at organisational level.

11. Affirmative action is still mostly seen as "a thing apart". It has not been integrated into the ongoing life and human resource practices of organisations. It is seen as something that only applies to black people (and sometimes women) – not as a process that affects the entire organisation and all its employees. Staffing opportunities that presented themselves when organisations were restructured were therefore often under-utilised, as affirmative action was viewed as being driven differently.

   While it is easy to spot the shortcomings of the efforts made by others, we have to recognise that these very problems are likely to occur in any organisation that embarks upon affirmative action. No matter how carefully an organisation strategises, communicates, implements and evaluates its policies and plans, the road will be bumpy and criticism will be levelled from all quarters. The intriguing question is why this is so.

   Affirmative action is seen by many as an historical necessity in South Africa and as a strategic imperative that makes good business sense. It also promotes the principles of equity and justice. At the same time, however, it is controversial, arouses mixed emotions and is difficult to implement.

   We want to argue that one can only understand this phenomenon by locating affirmative action within a wider societal and organisational context. This makes it possible to see that many of the problems commonly associated with affirmative action have been there all along. Affirmative action's crime – so to speak – is not that it encourages reverse discrimination or any of a number of oft-quoted criticisms. It is the fact that it is operating at a time when the labour market is undergoing considerable changes. The nature of work is changing – largely through the advances made by technology, especially information technology. Skill requirements are constantly adjusting themselves to new ways of organising and executing work, so that it is harder for everybody to get and keep jobs. We now talk about a "core" work-force and a "peripheral" work-force, with unemployment always on the increase. The idea of a "career" and what that means has thus changed radically over the last 50 years. It is within this context that we need to examine the common trends identified in the case studies.

   In this section we will examine three issues that underlie most of the problems identified above.

- Career paths for every employee.
- Negotiation and communication.
- Organisational culture.

CAREER PATHS FOR EVERYBODY

The notion that occupational mobility can be achieved through life-long learning, a term used all over the world, is increasingly being heard in South Africa within the broader framework of human resource development.

"Developing our human resources" is also one of the five major policy areas outlined in the Reconstruction and Development Programme and both education and training are emphasised as key issues. Policy proposals for an integrated approach to education and training, put forward by both the Congress of South African Trade Unions and the ANC, have been negotiated and adopted in the National Training Board's (1994) National Training Strategy Initiative. They also appear in the government's White Paper on Education.

The vision of an integrated education and training system that meets the economic and social needs of the country and the development needs of individuals promises increased access to learning and development opportunities for all South Africans. More flexible systems will offer modular courses, accreditation of prior experiential learning, credit accumulation and transfer.

While all this is laudable in social and political terms, we must also consider the matter in financial and organisational terms. The traditional characterisation of a "career" based on seniority and long service is being eroded by the pace of economic change. Organisations have to be prepared to change frequently and rapidly, which means that employers are less willing to make long-term commitments to individuals.

At the same time the new, flatter organisational structures reduce opportunities for hierarchical progression. Under the banner of "meritocracy", the responsibility for career development is increasingly being placed on the individual rather than the organisation. Individuals therefore actively need to seek progression through learning and experience, rather than think of promotion opportunities as steps up hierarchical ladders. Skill requirements for jobs are constantly changing and to enter, survive and progress in the labour market one has to keep on learning. Learning is not just something that is done before one starts working. The changing nature of work requires us to be life-long learners, not only to make progress but simply to meet the changing demands of current jobs.

In this regard, Watts[1] argues that individuals are moving more rapidly between educational institutions, between employers and between the two.

---

1. *Watts, AG. 1994. "Lifelong career development: towards a national strategy for career education and guidance", Occasional Paper, Careers Research and Advisory Centre, Cambridge.*

Their relationships with organisations are now more open to regular negotiation and review. If organisations are to take less responsibility for the long-term welfare of individuals they have to be more responsive to individuals' immediate needs and demands.

Individuals, on the other hand, have to take more responsibility for their own decisions and make more frequent career decisions. They therefore need to have access to career guidance throughout their learning and working lives.

It is evident that labour organisations, especially those that organise at the bottom end of the labour market, understand these issues well, in collective rather than individual terms. Their members are always the first to be affected by redundancy and retrenchment as they are deemed to have only generic and replaceable knowledge and skills. They are thus easily employed and easily dismissed. These trade unions argue that opportunities for life-long learning are essential to the democratic restructuring of the organisation of work. Even though the occupational status of the majority of workers may not change, they will be more competent, achieve higher productivity levels and, therefore, benefit through increased wages.

Current social changes are therefore eroding traditional middle-class notions of "a career" being the prerogative of the man who is the head of the family and the sole breadwinner. The racial segmentation of South African labour markets has further ensured that most jobs that offer reasonable job security, relatively high pay and opportunities for promotion have been held by white men.

Affirmative action plays a role in accelerating changes in both these societal conventions. A meaningful career is increasingly deemed possible for black and white, men and women – through either horizontal or vertical progression. Women and black men are, however, relative latecomers to the "career development" scene. For them it is crucial to be given opportunities for learning as well as opportunities to gain practical work experience. They push for internal staff development, rather than external recruitment.

The point, however, is that affirmative action did not supply the original impetus for occupational mobility, yet it often becomes a scapegoat for the way in which the labour market is changing. People blame affirmative action for the changes rather than realising that change is a central feature of the modern world. Economic and technological reasons are compelling many organisations to reduce the number of permanently employed staff and to operate in more flexible ways through the use of temporary and part-time workers. More people are therefore experiencing periods of under-employment. Affirmative action operates within this milieu, but it should not be viewed as the primary cause.

If this reality is acknowledged, then the barriers to progression that are implicit in many current organisational structures can be seen to demand critical attention. Organisations often stipulate matric or a degree or some other recognised qualification when they advertise a position. Such a requirement appears to be rational and reasonable. However, unless such a qualification adds value to the job in question, the requirement only places the entry or advancement requirements out of the reach of most black South Africans. This does not mean that formal qualifications should not be set as a requirement. They should be stipulated only where they bring a real advantage to the job in question. If a job is said to require a degree or formal qualification, it should be asked:

- What degree or qualification?
- How will this particular qualification enhance job performance?

Without doing this, an organisation can simply reproduce middle-class privilege. It can also do so by reserving certain jobs for particular groupings, or by keeping individuals tied to a particular job track without opportunities for job rotation and enrichment. It also makes nonsense of the promise of "meritocratic advancement for all" contained in mission statements.

NEGOTIATION AND COMMUNICATION

A consistent complaint made by employees in all the case studies was that communication about affirmative action was poor. Yet many organisations made an effort to create special communication channels, such as in-company videos, briefing sessions, conferences or workshops, to get the message across. They often did far more than they would normally do when communicating any other company policy. Why is it then that, despite these efforts, employees still complain that they do not know what is going on?

In our view, the explanation is found in the changes in the labour market discussed in the previous section. Affirmative action allows new groupings into previously narrowly regulated job categories. At the same time, organisations are restructuring and retrenching and there are fewer positions available for the greater number of people entering the job market. This means that there are more applicants or potential applicants competing for an ever-decreasing number of jobs.

Information about changes in staffing policies is of vital concern to everybody. While, for instance, changes in an organisation's marketing policy may affect the way in which people do their jobs, it does not necessarily affect their job security. Affirmative action is seen to do just that, thereby making some employees insecure and anxious, while others feel hopeful and optimistic.

Both groupings want access to what they consider to be "hard" information. By this they mean information about selection and advancement criteria and opportunities. Briefing sessions often convey the message in broad terms without being specific about the details. One of the reasons is that the underlying rationale for an affirmative action policy is not made explicit. Organisations do not necessarily want to hide their reasoning, but senior executives have often not debated the issue and developed a clear understanding of what they are committing themselves to. They have not established how it will work, how progress will be monitored and rewarded and how lack of progress will be penalised. The briefing session becomes a public relations exercise or an expression of intent and staff still do not know what is happening.

Closely related to the issue of communication are the complaints about lack of internal consultation and negotiation. Such complaints can be related to a greater global emphasis on democratic participation at all societal levels – be it the state, the work-place, the community or the family. What people are asking for is not only a set of clearly articulated policies and procedures, but a space to make their voices heard. The importance of seeing affirmative action as an ongoing process of communication, rather than as something which management decrees or sells, emerges forcefully.

Any organisation that wants to initiate affirmative action should understand that affirmative action affects every person in the organisation, and not only targeted categories such as black people and women. It is vital to the health of any organisation to ensure that the issue is thoroughly debated while the policy is developed so that views and opinions can be addressed up front. It is much more difficult to attempt to sell a completed affirmative action policy to a suspicious and apprehensive or, even worse, an apathetic work-force. All employees will ask the same question: "How is this going to affect my job and my future prospects in this organisation?"

Open consultation, negotiation and communication channels allow this to be a legitimate question, rather than something that is discussed informally. This is how "myths" are constructed and reproduced. Affirmative action is particularly vulnerable to myth-mongering and organisations consequently need to go to almost extraordinary lengths to promote transparency of both the process and the plan.

TRANSFORMING ORGANISATIONAL CULTURE

Culture is one of those complex terms that continually crops up in discussions about affirmative action. As individuals, we understand culture as socially and historically constructed frameworks for "making meaning" in our lives. What we deem to be our cultural orientation is a framework that enables us to establish our own identities. We therefore identify more easily with people with whom we share a cultural framework.

In South Africa, culture has often been equated with race, enabling us to construct myths about black cultures and white cultures as if they are light years apart. It is only fairly recently that we started realising that a white South African who grew up in Mowbray, Cape Town, has greater cultural affinity to a black South African who grew up a few miles away in Langa, Cape Town – even though apartheid laws kept them apart – than, for instance, an Italian person who grew up in Bologna, Italy. Apart from the biological fact that the Italian person also has a white skin, the white South African and the Italian may have been brought up under completely different social, political and economic conditions, thereby making them "strangers" to each other, without even a common South African identity.

Realising this does not, however, take away the reality of our divided South African society. We are only now starting to see South Africa as a country with 40 million people, black and white, men and women. This means that the now-fashionable notion of "affirming diversity" cannot be used as just another way of continuing to talk about white and black or male and female culture. It has to mean more than the reproduction of stereotypes, albeit with a bit more information-sharing about our daily work and private lives.

It is within this context that the transformation of organisational culture takes on a new meaning. The people who have been in an organisation the longest, with the most say in decision-making, obviously have had the strongest influence on shaping the ethos, customs and values of the organisation. When people talk about a white, male organisational culture they are referring to a historical reality. What this means is not that white males intentionally create an exclusive cultural space for themselves, but rather that they have always been able to make common assumptions about their white male counterparts. A few examples illustrate the point.

White men who attended middle-class schools usually played either rugby or cricket as part of their extra-mural activities. It is therefore natural that when they socialise at work they might talk about the latest rugby or cricket score. They do not realise that this may be an excluding conversation for women, who perhaps played netball or hockey, or for black men who played soccer. Talking about one's favourite sport is by no means inappropriate social behaviour, but when it is done in a work setting it somehow becomes an accepted part of organisational culture. Those people who cannot participate in the conversation do not feel themselves included in the "insider" group.

Many important decisions are made in the men's toilets, again excluding those who, by nature of social convention, use a separate set of toilets. It is also common practice for everyone in the organisation to continually refer to managers as "he". They do not realise that it is more inclusive to use she/he or to re-phrase the sentence so that a gender pronoun is avoided.

It might be part of an organisation's culture to have meetings early in the morning before the doors open for business. This is viewed as effective business practice, but it is also based on certain assumptions. These include the belief that everybody has access to company or private vehicles and reserved parking space, and that they can leave the house early without having to perform domestic duties or take children to school. When people to whom these assumptions do not apply attend these meetings, they may request that the meeting should start later or they may arrive late. If these people happen to be black or female, the comments that are often made are: "You see, they just don't have what it takes", or "they just don't care about productivity".

In the last example, a race or gender interpretation is given to a very real and practical situation. Those who have access to resources often find it difficult to see the barriers that exist for others. They see such conduct as an erosion of organisational culture, without thinking that maybe the organisational culture should be broadened to accommodate differences in people's practical realities as well as in their ideological orientations.

Transformation of organisational culture means that a traditional white male culture has to give way to a culture that respects difference and individuality. The objective, as Thomas[2] reminds us, is not to assimilate black people and women into a dominant white male culture, but "to create a dominant heterogeneous culture". The irony is that organisations have never consisted only of white males. There have always been black and women workers. What is different now, though, is that, through affirmative action, these groupings increasingly have access to decision-making and may now insist on equalising power.

What we are talking about here is not the "melting pot" metaphor that used to be so popular in America. We need to be multicultural rather than culture-blind. In practical terms, there is a range of issues that organisations have to attend to once they embark on the affirmative action route. In the end it all boils down to democratic, transparent and inclusive human resource practices, but it may be helpful to single out two relevant areas.

LANGUAGE

Organisations usually choose one language as the official language of spoken and written communication inside the company, although they may communicate with customers in more languages. If, for instance, this language is English, it means that English first-language speakers have an implicit advantage when they speak or write.

Once an organisation accepts multilingualism as both a reality and an advantage in the market place, it should be included in its merit criteria. A black person therefore does not just get the position because the organisation wishes to meet affirmative action targets. Instead, the person may have a material advantage over other candidates who can offer only one language.

It is, however, no use declaring multilingualism as a merit criterion without ensuring that the organisation accommodates more than one language in both its internal and external communication. First-language speakers of English are often highly offended if they cannot understand what is being said. They take it for granted that all communication should be in English and they see other people as somehow deficient if they cannot express themselves easily in English. What they fail to realise is that, according to the multilingual merit criterion, they themselves are the ones who are deficient.

An organisation that prides itself on being able to serve a customer in the language of her/his choice needs to ensure that the staff who make this choice possible should also be able to express themselves in their first language in the organisation. This does not mean that we should all be able to speak 11

2. Thomas, J. and R. Roosevelt. 1990. "From affirmative action to affirming diversity", in Harvard Business Review, *March-April.*

languages, but rather that we should develop a culture of acknowledgement and respect for languages which we do not speak.

Most people do speak English, but the elitism that is attached to an Oxbridge accent does not have a place in South Africa. There seems to be little point in affirming diversity, then still favouring a particular way of speaking English. Second-language speakers sometimes forget an English word or do not know it. It is then helpful if it is acceptable to say the word in one's first language and get somebody else to translate. This is often considered acceptable for foreigners but not for our fellow South Africans.

Many people say that language is only a means of communication and that it should not be an issue. Languages are, however, also a way of expressing our identities and it is therefore vital to make multilingualism an accepted part of organisational culture.

TRADITION

Acknowledging multiculturalism implies careful re-evaluation of all kinds of organisational traditions. This includes accepting that not all employees think that "having a drink with the boys in the pub" is a fun thing to do. It is also important to understand that employees may wish to observe different religious holidays and respect different historic events as public holidays. Even the food that is served at organisational functions needs to accommodate different eating requirements, such as halal, kosher or vegetarian.

WHERE TO FROM HERE?

Where will it all end if we have to accommodate everybody's individual preferences and whims? This is the question that frequently arises. The issue at stake here is not individual preferences, but the ability to manage an organisation without advantages or disadvantages for any member of the diverse work-force. This means that we have to scrutinise every human resource policy and activity to ensure that there is not a hidden inclusion-exclusion assumption. Thomas[3] argues that affirmative action is an "artificial and transitional, but necessary, stage on the road to a truly diverse work-force".

If that is our goal then we must address issues that set particular groupings at a disadvantage. We must also ensure that existing organisational policies and activities do not entrench this disadvantage in tacit and unspoken ways. Embarking on affirmative action means more than opening up access and promoting a few individuals on the grounds of affirmative action. If affirmative action is accepted as a sound business and moral strategy, then all members of

---

3. *Thomas, J. and R. Roosevelt. 1990. "From affirmative action to affirming diversity", in* Harvard Business Review, *March-April: 117.*

the work-force actively need to work towards transforming the organisational culture. At one level, this means that all formal human resource policies and practices must be stripped of terms and conditions that discriminate against any particular grouping. Equitable and explicit criteria must be articulated for each job or occupational level. However, as the discussion clearly shows, it means more than that. It means that the whole organisation has to become an affirmative action organisation. Employees need to feel that their future prospects have been taken into consideration during the policy development stage, and every appointment or promotion thereafter must be conducted in terms of the policy. Only then will affirmative action be integrated into the life of the organisation, rather than remain an artificial, transitional stage that never reaches conclusion.

In the next chapter, practical steps are offered for the development, implementation and review of an affirmative action policy. The process suggested follows the natural cycle of any strategic plan, but it stresses participation by everybody in the organisation in a manageable way. The process will, in itself, have a powerful effect on the transformation of organisational culture. It will also go a long way towards ensuring that affirmative action organisations become a South African reality. ∎

PART THREE

THE WORKBOOK

CHAPTER 4

CREATING YOUR OWN AFFIRMATIVE ACTION PROCESS

INTRODUCTION

The purpose of this chapter is to assist your organisation in the formulation of an affirmative action policy and to ensure the successful implementation of the approach you develop. A range of "affirmative action policy blueprints" have been published in South Africa, most of which provide useful ideas and suggestions that may be copied in other organisations. However, the successful implementation of affirmative action requires the careful consideration of the specific history and context of the organisation.

This chapter will assist you in constructing your own context-specific affirmative action policy by providing:

- Guidelines on how to establish a consultative process.
- A framework to construct and conduct an audit of human resource practices in your organisation, with a view to identifying problems and alternative practices which support affirmative action.
- Guidelines to develop a policy document.
- Broad guidelines on policy implementation. By the end of the chapter, you should be in a position to formulate a policy document for your organisation based on consultation, discussion and debate. You should also be in a position to monitor, review and improve the process over time.

GUIDING PRINCIPLES

Before turning to the process of developing an affirmative action policy, it is useful to reflect on three important principles raised in Chapter Three. These principles have guided our approach to this chapter.

BUSINESS STRATEGY

To succeed affirmative action should be directly linked to business strategy. The implication is that the organisation has to clearly define, debate and integrate the links between strategic direction and affirmative action.

HUMAN RESOURCE DEVELOPMENT

Affirmative action is most successful when it is planned and implemented as an integral part of human resource development. Given the potential for explicit and systemic discriminatory policies and practices, affirmative action policy formation should begin by re-evaluating all existing human resource policies and practices.

IMPORTANCE OF CONSULTATION

Affirmative action policy development requires special emphasis on wide consultation. Although the trend in the 1980s was to develop affirmative action strategies with little or no consultation, there has been a distinct shift in the 1990s. Organisations are increasingly realising the value of consulting those people for whom affirmative action is intended. They also realise the need to more openly address the anxiety that is likely to emerge as a result of affirmative action programmes. The process of consultation should ideally involve all stakeholders in the organisation. It should be aimed at establishing a common understanding of the intentions, possibilities and limitations presented by the organisational culture and structure.

POLICY DEVELOPMENT

The remainder of this chapter sets out a process for developing an affirmative action policy for your organisation. This process offers a series of steps for linking affirmative action to your strategic direction. To achieve this requires a thorough evaluation of human resource practices, preferably conducted through a process of consultation.

Over and above conforming to these three principles, your organisation will be able to generate and choose its own options. The process followed can be summarised as follows:

DEBATE AND ACCEPTANCE AT BOARD LEVEL

SET UP TASK GROUP

CONDUCT HUMAN RESOURCE AUDIT

- Construct employment profile by race, gender and level
- Review human resource policies and practices

FORMULATE HUMAN RESOURCE REPORT AND POLICY

IMPLEMENT, MONITOR AND REVIEW POLICY

Each of these steps are discussed below.

BOARD LEVEL ACCEPTANCE

The first stage in developing an affirmative action strategy is for the board or management structure of the organisation to understand the importance and benefits of affirmative action. This recognition may be prompted by a combination of the internal/external factors mentioned in Chapter Three. This realisation should be accompanied by an open debate at board level, which should include a consideration of the state of organisational readiness and institutional constraints. In those organisations that have already implemented some form of affirmative action, it is important to debate and review that experience and to isolate the critical factors for future success.

It is often due to insufficient clarity at board level that policies are inadequate and implementation fails. Unless the rationale for affirmative action is clearly understood and articulated at board level, it is impossible for the policy to be implemented.

Once the board has reached sufficient consensus on the need for affirmative action, it has to allocate resources (time, staff and money) and choose the most appropriate consultative process. Each of the case studies show that the absence of consultation makes implementation difficult and controversial.

One option is for the board to manage the consultation process itself. This would require each board member to take responsibility for a functional area or division in the organisation and set up forums for discussion and debate. This makes the board accessible and clearly demonstrates its commitment to affirmative action. Although commendable, the disadvantage of this approach is that board members may not have the time to devote to this demanding and lengthy process.

A more practical option is for the board to set up a task group and delegate to it the responsibility for policy development. This task group should include representatives of all races, genders and levels in the organisation, as well as the core interest groups such as staff associations, trade unions and management. In the interests of legitimacy, it is important that the existence and creation of the task group is negotiated, and its members not simply appointed by the board or management.

SET UP TASK GROUP

MANDATE

The task group's mandate may range from a policy advice group to responsibility for setting and implementing policy, although it is more likely to be the former. Whatever the brief, it is important that the task group is given the resources, independence and authority to meet its mandate. These requirements are important to ensure that the task group is not reduced to a "lobby group" or perceived to be a "management committee".

▨ REPORTING

The task group should report directly to the board, which will ultimately approve the policy. Reporting should be done at regular, stipulated intervals to ensure that the board remains in touch with the process and is able to contribute to the thinking along the way.

▨ RESOURCES

All task group members should be formally relieved from core job responsibilities to meet their objectives. The task group should be allocated a budget commensurate with its brief.

▨ COMPOSITION AND SIZE

The task group should be sufficiently representative of race, gender and decision-making levels. As a general guideline, a task group of between eight and 12 people is ideal.

▨ RESPONSIBILITIES

The task group has three key responsibilities:
- to draft a "statement of intent" which should cover the motivation, aims and terms of reference;
- to commission or conduct an audit of permanent staff strength by race, gender and level, as well as an in-depth review of human resource practices in the organisation;
- to draft the organisation's affirmative action policy based on the results of this audit.

The most time-consuming and important of the task group's activities is conducting or commissioning the human resource audit. The audit process is dealt with in detail below.

CONDUCT HUMAN RESOURCE AUDIT

WHAT IS AN AUDIT?

An audit is not simply an accounting exercise. Rather, it is a reflective mechanism to help the organisation clarify where it is now. It also identifies the internal factors that will inhibit/support the implementation of its affirmative action strategy.

The two major components of the audit are:
- A detailed employment profile of the organisation's employees by race, gender and skills levels. This should be conducted at an organisational

level, as well as by division and functional area, if appropriate.
- An in-depth review of current human resource practices in the organisation, and staff members' experiences and perceptions of these practices.

SUGGESTED AUDIT METHODOLOGY

The audit involves the collection of information from as many people as possible in the organisation. There are a number of ways in which this could be done, including focus groups, questionnaires, one-on-one interviews, etc. The task group will need to carefully consider which method is most suitable given the size, structure and culture of the organisation.

It is generally agreed that focus groups are the best way in which to gather the audit information. A focus group is a selected, diverse group of people who are brought together to discuss and make recommendations on specific organisational issues.

FOCUS GROUPS ARE THE PREFERRED OPTION BECAUSE:

- Each of the case studies clearly shows that the degree of consultation and involvement in establishing an affirmative action policy is critical to its success. The problem in large organisations is that the number and geographical spread of employees does not allow information to be collected individually from all the employees. Focus groups are therefore practical mechanisms to meet the tension between effective involvement and organisation size.
- Owing to the perceptions and emotions surrounding affirmative action, any plan perceived to be imposed by any one interest group is likely to fail. If focus group representatives are nominated across race, gender, level and interest group, these individuals are more likely to be accepted as representative. This, in turn, will validate the findings.
- Focus groups are an effective means of gathering the depth of information required for affirmative action decision-making. By involving a group of people from diverse backgrounds, different insights and experiences of the same organisational practices will emerge. Furthermore, discussion in focus groups allows for greater clarification of data than is possible in questionnaires.
- Given that focus group activity is interactive, it allows for the building of ideas and synthesis along the way.
- Affirmative action is a contentious issue. As different groups begin to discuss and exchange their perceptions, they are encouraged to question their own

assumptions. This will assist with creating the common ground needed to facilitate the implementation phase.

Although the use of focus groups has many benefits, it is also important to point out the disadvantages of this approach.

- The process is time consuming and can be costly.
- In the absence of skilled facilitation, focus groups can degenerate into a general complaints session or non-focused discussion.
- Some people may feel too inhibited or uncomfortable to participate openly in cross-sectional groups.

Bearing each of these reservations in mind, the focus group route best ensures a process characterised by involvement, quality of information and legitimacy. The reservations can largely be overcome through careful planning and scheduling, the selection of appropriately skilled facilitator(s) and the thorough communication of the aims of the process to all staff.

The decision to use focus groups, or another appropriate form of rigorous consultation, should be based on the organisational culture and structure. Whichever method you choose, the content of the process should focus on the sections and questions that follow.

PRACTICAL CONSIDERATIONS IN SETTING UP FOCUS GROUPS

- Focus groups should represent a cross section of the organisation and include diversity by race, gender and skill levels in each group. Participant groups should preferably not mirror normal working groups as individuals may not be able to discuss issues openly in the company of their superiors.
- Proper briefings prior to attendance is essential. For example, a letter explaining the purpose and process should be sent to each participant. Individuals should have the choice of participating or not.
- The following ground rules should be made explicit to ensure open discussion:
  - confidentiality;
  - no victimisation;
  - open and frank discussion;
  - discussion to focus on the issues, not the people;
  - equal participation, regardless of level.
  These and/or additional ground rules need to be accepted by the group.
- The ideal size is between 10 and 25 people.
- The number of focus groups will depend on the size of the organisation. The ideal situation would be to have everyone in the organisation participating in one of the focus groups. In small organisations of up to 300 employees this is possible. In medium-sized organisations (300 to 1 000 employees), a

sample of staff would need to be selected for participation. In large organisations (over 1 000 employees) sampled focus group activity may be supplemented with questionnaires and/or interviews. These may use a combination of closed and open-ended questions structured along the lines of the focus group discussions.

- In smaller focus groups, facilitation could be conducted in plenary sessions only, but in larger groups it is advisable to combine small group work with plenary sessions.
- Internal and/or external facilitators can be used. The benefit of using an outside facilitator is the perception of impartiality. A difficulty may be their lack of insight into some of the internal nuances. Using an internal facilitator helps to build commitment and ownership of the process. It is suggested that outside facilitators are used only if the organisation lacks internal facilitation skills or requires expert assistance to aid the design of the process.
- The focus group discussions need not cover all human resource practices but should, at least, cover those directly related to recruitment, selection, promotion, grievance and disciplinary procedures, performance evaluation, staff development/training and organisational culture.
- The facilitator(s) should carefully explain how the information collected will be synthesised into a report, the purpose of the report and the feedback process to participants.

GUIDELINES FOR CONDUCTING A HUMAN RESOURCE AUDIT

PHASE ONE
This involves information gathering and analysis. In this phase, you are required to collect data on your entire work-force by race, gender and level. The purpose for doing this is to create an employment profile that gives you a clear picture of your present staff composition. This will inform priorities for change. Over and above this stock data, it is important to collect information about recruitment, promotion and exit patterns. This flow data will help to identify mobility patterns and opportunities in your organisation as a basis for informed human resource planning.

PHASE TWO
This involves a detailed review of human resource policies and practices conducted within the focus groups. The focus groups should begin by reviewing the stock and flow data collected in order to understand the outcome of current practice. The detailed review should focus on identifying the obstacles and opportunities that each human resource practice presents for the implementation of affirmative action.
The recommended human resource review process is presented as follows:
- A statement of purpose for each human resource practice and a short

discussion of some of the common problems elicited from the case studies.
- A set of questions aimed at assessing the extent to which existing policies and practices inhibit or support an affirmative action strategy. The questions are aimed at helping the focus group facilitator(s) guide the discussions. The answers generated from the questions should form the basis of the report and draft policy presented to the board by the task group.

RECRUITMENT

AIM

The aim of recruitment is for the organisation to attract as many suitable external applicants for a post as possible. In an affirmative action context this means a comprehensive recruitment strategy that ensures that people from all communities are reached, especially those that are under-represented in the organisation.

COMMON PROBLEM AREAS

While many organisations recognise the importance of internal development, they often resort to external appointments as a "quick fix" to filling vacancies. This occurs either because they have not invested sufficiently in preparing people for future job prospects, or because their training is not linked to business development. A recruitment plan that involves introducing fresh perspectives and internal development will help the organisation to grow beyond the homogeneous culture that develops when it only grooms and promotes from within.

Once a decision has been made to recruit externally, it is necessary to spread the net as widely as possible and to ensure access to the target affirmative action constituencies. Often appointments are filled by word of mouth, that is through networks rather than by making use of the public media. It is also common for organisations to advertise only in newspapers that are read by a small proportion of the population or to place advertisements only in a single language, in most cases English. Furthermore, organisations often use only one recruitment agency for all their placements thus relying on the networks of that agency only. These practices serve to limit the scope and scale of individuals attracted to apply for vacancies.

RECRUITMENT AUDIT QUESTIONS

These are the questions you should ask your human resource department, and the focus groups, to assess whether your current recruitment practice does/does not support an affirmative action strategy.

1. Briefly describe the organisation's recruitment process.
2. What media is predominantly used?
3. Review the organisation's recruitment patterns by race, gender and skill level over the past one to three years.
4. Who is responsible for recruitment in your organisation by race, gender and skill level?
5. Does the recruitment team have the requisite knowledge and skills to ensure that they are successfully reaching all the communities/target groups you would want to attract?

SELECTION

AIM

The aim of selection is to identify the most suitable candidate for a vacant position in the organisation. In general, South African organisations rely on two selection methods: interviewing and testing. The common pitfalls of each are discussed below.

COMMON PROBLEM AREAS

Given South African organisational structures, interviewers have traditionally been white managers. They are usually chosen as interviewers on the basis of their job competence and managerial status and not because they are trained and skilled interviewers/selectors. The racial and gender composition of interview panels therefore tends to support what is referred to as "homosocial reproduction". This is the tendency of selectors to see the greatest potential in those that are similar to themselves. At the very least, "other" candidates are inhibited or threatened by such selection panels or interviewers.

A second problem area is the specification of selection criteria. Implicit or explicit criteria are often not related to job competencies and this may exclude the broader pool of potential candidates. For example, many advertisements stress the maximum requirements for the job with a particularly heavy accent on formal education and interactive skills. Many South Africans have been denied formal work or educational opportunities, but may have developed skills through alternative learning avenues.

Similarly, selection criteria often tend to concentrate on a candidate's current ability to do a job rather than their future potential to do the job or their ability to learn a job. Potential is more difficult to assess and reinforces the necessity to train selectors, appoint diverse selection panels and recognise prior learning or related competencies. The difference between potential and skill is that the former recognises the possibility of acquiring the capacity for the job through training.

Many organisations in South Africa rely on psychometric testing (which focuses on intellect, interests and personality) and assessment without measuring the validity of these tests in their particular organisation. The fundamental concern is whether testing persons whose backgrounds are different from the group that set the test standards is valid. In South Africa, it is argued that this is particularly so for tests that measure intellectual abilities, which are a direct product of the benefits of one's educational experience, opportunities and exposure. With the historically low educational standards for blacks, the tests currently used may not prove good predictors of future performance.

Personality tests cover the traits, habits and family background of a candidate in order to provide a picture of the unconscious forces shaping his/her makeup. These tests can serve as a reliable indicator of how a person would fit into the organisational culture and environment. It is inappropriate, however, to use these tests as indicators of ability or potential. Information gained from personality tests could alternatively be derived from well-structured interviews.

Information gleaned from psychometric testing is not informative and meaningful unless the tests have been validated in the organisation, are culturally neutral and are used for the purpose for which they were designed. The successful application of tests also requires skilled users who understand the cultural context of the candidate. This standard remains a concern.

SELECTION AUDIT QUESTIONS

These are the questions you should ask your human resource department, and the focus groups, in order to assess whether your current selection policy and practice does/does not support an affirmative action strategy.

1. Review the organisation's selection and placement patterns over the past three years by race, gender and skill level.

2. Who is currently responsible for selection in your organisation by race, gender and skill level?

3. Do these selectors have sufficient insight into, and experience with, the communities/target groups you would want to attract?

4. Describe the organisation's present selection process (types of interviews, types of testing, etc).

5. Are these methods biased against target groups in any way?

6. Have the tests you use been evaluated against long-term performance in your organisation?

7. What suggestions do you have for alternative or complementary selection methods?

INDUCTION

AIM

The purpose of induction is to orientate and integrate new recruits. The aim is to assist the person to get up to speed as soon as possible in their department or work unit. They should also understand how their work relates to the total organisation.

COMMON PROBLEM AREAS

Traditionally, organisations wait for the accumulation of a group of new recruits before they run an induction programme. This delays the induction process for earlier recruits. Furthermore, induction programmes are often generic programmes facilitated by the human resource department. They are seldom customised to the individual's work needs, entry point and starting knowledge base. The tendency to run generic programmes does not allow the person most familiar with the new recruits' responsibilities – his/her manager – to be involved in the design and implementation of the induction programme.

INDUCTION AUDIT QUESTIONS

These are the questions you should ask your human resource department, and the focus groups, in order to assess whether your current recruitment practice does/does not support an affirmative action strategy.

1. Does your organisation have an induction process for new recruits?

2. Is it available for all new recruits?

3. Who is responsible for induction?

4. How soon after entry does induction take place?

5. Do you evaluate your induction procedures?

6. Is your induction programme customised to the individual and his/her entry level job?

7. Suggestions for improving induction in the organisation.

TRAINING

This section refers to training both post-induction and for on-going staff development.

AIM

The aim of training is to provide access and opportunity for people throughout the organisation to develop skills to meet changing work processes, future job prospects and the overall business strategy.

COMMON PROBLEM AREAS

Traditionally, in South Africa, training has enjoyed tenuous links with business performance. The result is that training is often not linked to organisational performance, job performance or personal development. One of the reasons for this is that training is often conducted by human resource personnel without any design input from line management.

Furthermore, individual training may also not be linked to performance on the job or preparation for additional responsibility or a future job prospect. Where training has been provided, there is often no evaluation of how it has affected performance. This results in high-cost, low-impact training.

Individuals are also often not consulted about their training needs. This may prevent them from understanding the motivation for training, or from contributing to the choice/design of training programmes. This may impact on the employees' commitment to training and the extent to which the individual benefits from it.

A related problem is that often black recruits are not given sufficient responsibility and are instead subjected to an endless cycle of training. This was particularly the case during the 1980s, when it was common practice to set up separate training programmes for black people. This helped to stigmatise training and reinforced negative perceptions of black ability. This is to not to say that in certain instances black people or women may not need specialised training. But one cannot assume that this applies to all blacks and/or women and never applies to white men. As with all training, the approach should be to base training on individual needs as they relate to organisational priorities.

Many medium and large organisations in South Africa are realising the importance of training for achieving long-term goals and have set aside large budgets to implement training on an annual basis. Unfortunately, budget allocations are often skewed towards managerial and supervisory training and do not make provision for skills development lower down the organisation.

TRAINING AUDIT QUESTIONS

These are the questions you should ask your human resource department, and the focus groups, in order to assess whether your current training policy and practice does/does not support an affirmative action strategy.

1. What is the organisation's current annual training budget?
2. What type of training is taking place and who gets access to training by race, gender and skill level?
3. Who is responsible for selecting people for training in your organisation? What skills do they have and what criteria are predominantly used?
4. How is training in your organisation linked to key business imperatives?
5. What recognition or credit is given to training and how is training linked to advancement/promotion?
6. Are your trainers sufficiently skilled in training a diverse work-force?
7. Are line managers involved in the design and delivery of training?

PROMOTION AND PERFORMANCE RECOGNITION

AIM
The purpose of promotion is to fill vacancies in the organisation, reward performance and provide development opportunities.

COMMON PROBLEM AREAS
Internal promotions are used to reward people for performance and give them opportunities for further development. As many organisations realise the need to change their race and gender profile they are tempted to appoint external black people and women immediately into management positions, rather than to identify and develop internal potential.

Alternatively, if promotion and development opportunities have not been systematically planned, external appointments become necessary. This route of "quick-fix" external promotions often provides no more than a short-term window dressing benefit. External appointees may not have the necessary training and/or are not provided with the required support. Over and above this reservation, an over-reliance on external promotion affects internal loyalty and commitment and prevents a development culture being established.

A further issue is that promotion is often viewed in an organisation as the ultimate marker of personal development. The reality is that at more senior levels in an organisation, there are few positions available. This means that alternative and more creative mechanisms for development need to be considered. Some of these alternative development options may include incremental responsibility, job enrichment, job rotation and secondments to project teams, etc.

Promotion and development policies also do not consider the barriers to the movement of people across skill levels. For example, this applies to the movement of labourers to operating positions or the movement of supervisors to management.

Given that promotion involves a selection process, it is also subject to the same difficulties mentioned in the discussion on selection.

PROMOTION AND RECOGNITION AUDIT QUESTIONS

These are the questions you should ask your human resource department, and focus groups, to assess whether your current training policy and practice does/does not support an affirmative action programme.

1. Review the organisation's promotion patterns over the last three years by race, gender and level.
2. Review the promotion criteria on which basis people are promoted in the organisation?
3. Are these criteria accepted as relevant and fair throughout the organisation?
4. Who is responsible for making promotion decisions?
5. What is the link between performance management and promotion?
6. What are the barriers to promotion in the organisation (race, gender, level, etc)?
7. What is the effect of organisational structure on promotion and development opportunities?
8. Are there alternative avenues for development, other than promotion, in your organisation?

CULTURE/WORK ENVIRONMENT

AIM

Culture is difficult to define. It is commonly referred to as "the way we do things around here" and presents itself as the unwritten ground rules that govern organisational practices and individual behaviour.

COMMON PROBLEM AREAS

It is not possible to implement affirmative action successfully without considering the extent to which the organisational culture/work environment either inhibits or facilitates the process. Unless the environment in the organisation is supportive, it is likely to undermine the affirmative action initiatives.

Although the organisation's mission statement and individual employees may espouse a particular dominant culture, culture in use presents a different reality. Organisations often implement affirmative action without acknowledging the impact that the dominant culture has on its success, particularly the impact that it has on the integration of new recruits.

Furthermore, organisations have many sub-cultures, some of which will inhibit, and some of which will support, affirmative action. Affirmative action is often implemented on the basis of an assumption about the dominant culture without a sufficient understanding of the impact and influence that sub-cultures will have on the programme.

Although an organisation's culture may seem immutable, cultures are dynamic and may be influenced over time. Affirmative action will in itself introduce a greater diversity of people as well as new sub-cultures. It is important therefore for organisations to allow for a more diverse work-force to influence the dominant and sub-cultures in the organisation.

CULTURE/WORK ENVIRONMENT AUDIT QUESTIONS

These are the questions you should ask your human resource department, and the focus groups, in order to assess whether your current culture/sub-culture(s) does/does not support an affirmative action strategy.

1. Describe the current culture(s): Ask for key words from each member.
2. Which of these cultures is perceived as the dominant culture?
3. Group the key words into those that facilitate or inhibit affirmative action implementation.
4. Group the inhibiting factors into those that can be overcome in the short term and those that can only be overcome in the long term.
5. Document suggested solutions.

CONFLICT RESOLUTION

AIM
The purpose of conflict resolution procedures in an organisation is to voice and resolve problems in a fair and transparent way.

COMMON PROBLEM AREAS
Race and gender discrimination are criminal offences in South Africa. However, many organisations have yet to integrate non-discriminatory codes into their formal disciplinary procedures.

Even where mechanisms exist to deal with overt discrimination, few organisations have begun to think creatively about how to create channels to deal with covert and/or systemic discrimination. The latter is difficult to prove and, as a result, there are often no mechanisms to address this discrimination before it develops into a formal grievance.

CONFLICT RESOLUTION AUDIT QUESTIONS

These are the questions you should ask your human resource department, and the focus groups, in order to assess whether your current grievance or disciplinary procedure does/does not support an affirmative action strategy.

1. Does your organisation specifically cater for race and gender discrimination in its disciplinary and grievance procedures?
2. Who has used these procedures by race, gender and job level and what types of complaints are raised?
3. What alternative mechanisms exist for dealing with issues of discrimination?
4. What are the most common forms of overt and systemic discrimination in your organisation?
5. What mechanisms can you suggest for dealing with overt and systemic discrimination?

OTHER OPTIONS

You may wish, in addition to the standard audit, to discuss with your focus groups creative options for introducing and supporting affirmative action in your organisation. The list below offers some ideas used by South African organisations that you may wish to consider.
- Source a sizeable percentage of your outside purchases from black and women-owned businesses.
- Joint ventures with black and women-owned firms.

- Increase your notice period for managerial staff to give you more time to find suitable black/women replacements. Ensure that a condition of leaving is to train new people. This would apply only to voluntary exits from the organisation.
- Sponsor African language programmes for all staff (compulsory attendance could be another option).
- Formal contact with township communities, schools and civic organisations.
- Briefings and/or internal debates for all staff on political, social and business developments.
- Include the locally dominant African language in the organisation's signage.

HUMAN RESOURCE REPORT AND POLICY FORMULATION

Once the audit is completed, the task group needs to translate the audit findings into a human resource report. This report provides the basis for the development of a draft affirmative action policy. Both of these documents must be presented to the board for discussion and adoption.

The structure which follows is a suggestion on how to put together your findings. The appendix provides four examples of affirmative action policies adapted from organisations in South Africa.

HUMAN RESOURCE REPORT

The following sub-categories may be useful in structuring your report.

▨ **STATISTICAL BACKGROUND**
- Current staff profile: race, gender and levels.
- Recruitment, promotion and exit patterns.
- Training and development expenditure by race, gender and skill levels.
This information should be available from your human resource department or the individual that deals with personnel administration. If not, this information should be collated and analysed as a project.

▨ **PERCEPTIONS, PROBLEMS AND SUGGESTIONS FOR IMPROVING CURRENT HUMAN RESOURCES PRACTICES**
The guideline presented below is a suggestion for structuring your findings:
- A description of current practice (recruitment, selection, induction, etc).
- An analysis of how each human resource practice currently promotes or inhibits the implementation of affirmative action.
- Suggested changes to each human resource practice to ensure the effective implementation of affirmative action.

DRAFT AFFIRMATIVE ACTION POLICY

The following sub-categories may be useful in structuring your policy document.

▨ **RATIONALE FOR AFFIRMATIVE ACTION**
The following reasons are commonly found in South African policy documents:
- **ECONOMIC** — It makes good economic sense to match your consumer profile with your staff profile. Economic growth in South Africa will require organisations to assume a major responsibility for overcoming

skills shortages by training and developing all human resources.

- **MORAL** — South African organisations are obliged to contribute towards providing opportunities and access to those denied opportunities during apartheid. This responsibility assists with reconciliation and reconstruction at the national level.
- **MANAGEMENT AND HUMAN RESOURCE PRACTICES** — South African management and human resource practices are rated very poorly in terms of international competitiveness. Competitiveness and organisational performance in South Africa therefore depend critically on a review of management practices and particularly human resource practice.
- **LEGISLATION** — Given political change in South Africa, most organisations are expecting some form of legislative intervention designed to stimulate and monitor affirmative action. Those organisations that seriously engage in affirmative action now will be in a better position to deal with legislation, whatever form it takes.

DEFINITION AND OBJECTIVES

A definition of affirmative action should clearly specify the aim of the policy, identify the target groups and the methods that will be employed to meet these objectives.

Affirmative action is generally considered to incorporate a series of measures designed to create equal opportunity without adversely affecting the broader career opportunities within the organisation.

South African target groups are generally considered to be black people and women at all levels of the organisation. Many United States and European-based firms also include the disabled as a target group. There is some debate as to whether the target group should include coloureds and Asians as well as Africans. This indicates the need to consider current staff profiles and the population of the region before making a decision. In the process of negotiating target groups, it is important to consider the balance between development into and at management levels. There should also be a longer term investment in the development of employees lower down in the organisation.

GOALS AND TIMETABLES

- Quotas are fixed targets and often set without considering the future staffing opportunities in the organisation. Goals are specific targets for the race and gender composition of the work-force to be met in specified time frames. They are decided internally on the basis of organisational opportunity and need to be regularly reviewed on the basis of progress.
- Goals should be organisation specific and take into account a realistic review of future staffing opportunities. Future staffing capacity should consider organisational growth or decline, retrenchments, retirements, staff turnover, current skill base in the organisation and any restructuring initiatives envisaged.
- Goals should also take into account an assessment of the skills available

in the external labour market.

- Goals should include targets and timetables differentiated by race, gender and skill level in the organisation.
- Goals should distinguish between the long term or the termination point of the policy and the incremental steps required to get there.

ROLES AND RESPONSIBILITIES

The key actors in the implementation of affirmative action are the chief executive, task group, line management and human resource department.

- **EXECUTIVE RESPONSIBILITY** — Executive responsibility for affirmative action should lie with the chief executive.
- **CHAMPION ROLE** — The chief executive may take responsibility for driving the process. Alternatively, this task could be devolved to either the task group, or an appointed senior person with sufficient authority and credibility who has this as his/her sole responsibility. We do not recommend that this driving role be devolved to the human resource department which fulfils a service function and is not directly responsible for the management of staff. However, the role of the human resources department as a technical adviser is invaluable.
- **ADVISORY ROLE** — If the task group is retained beyond policy development, it should assist with the development and implementation of the policy together with the person driving the policy. Key human resource personnel may function as a professional advisory group. It is recommended that the task group is retained for the implementation phase as this representative grouping is uniquely placed to provide advice.
- **OPERATIONAL ROLE** — This responsibility incorporates managing and developing staff and ensuring a non-discriminatory environment. This responsibility should fall to line management as they are directly concerned with managing staff. Again, human resources personnel could assist in a professional support role.
- **MONITORING AND EVALUATION** — Responsibility for this task should be divided. Human resources staff should maintain the human resource database and track trends in promotion, recruitment, staff profiles and training. Direct monitoring and reporting to the board may be done by the executive director or his/her nominee or the task group, whoever is responsible for the champion role. If the task group is to perform the direct monitoring role it must be given board level authority to perform this role.

IMPLEMENTATION, MONITORING AND REVIEW

The next phase, implementation, is about making affirmative action work. Once the policy has been presented to the board, edited and ratified, it must be communicated throughout the organisation and implemented with clear accountability.

COMMUNICATION

It is essential that everyone in the organisation is introduced to the policy and has the opportunity to ask any questions of clarification or raise any concerns. It is suggested that the process should start with the chief executive briefing his/her senior management. Each senior manager should then be responsible for formally introducing the policy to all staff in each division in a personal presentation which may be prepared by the task group. It is a good idea to hold these communication sessions in each division on the same day to avoid misinterpretation and mixed messages.

Each person in the company should also receive a policy document and a letter from the chief executive formally endorsing the strategy. Formal channels should also be created to allow individual staff members to approach the task group on any questions of clarification. For those organisations that are internally electronically linked, communication may be enhanced by the establishment of a computerised affirmative action bulletin board.

ACCOUNTABILITY

The chief executive is ultimately responsible for the successful implementation of affirmative action. It is important, however, to ensure that affirmative action is considered equal to any other strategic organisational objective. Its successful implementation should be subject to the same rewards or sanctions. Affirmative action must become one of the key performance criteria for each manager. This means that each manager's performance review, and the financial rewards attached to this, will be directly related to his or her contribution to affirmative action.

MONITORING

The affirmative action task group should be responsible for designing a monitoring and reporting format. This reporting format should then be made available to individual divisions or departments, which then become responsible for reporting progress on implementation plans on a quarterly basis. The chief executive or the task group should present consolidated progress reports on implementation plans to the board.

The following should be included in progress reports:

- **PROGRESS AGAINST SPECIFIC OBJECTIVES:**
  - Staff profile changes against objectives/targets.
  - Flow data: recruitment, promotions and exits by skill level, race and gender.
  - Opportunities created through training and education by skill level, race and gender.

- **PERCEPTIONS**
  These may be generated from interviews with critical people driving the affirmative action process. These include representatives of senior management, line management, new target group recruits, black and women managers, clerical staff, shop floor and union members. The interviews should focus on:
  - performance of blacks and other target groups;
  - obstacles to implementation;
  - management support;
  - commitment of target groups;
  - internal work environment;
  - successes;
  - suggestions for improvement.

- **REVIEW**
  An important objective in monitoring is the capacity to feed the results of the monitoring exercise into a review of the original plan. Where specific problems are identified, they should be addressed by the task group or, if serious enough, project teams may be commissioned to find solutions. In this way, affirmative action is an ongoing process which, like any other business strategy, continually aims to improve.

APPENDIX

AFFIRMATIVE
ACTION POLICY
DOCUMENTS

EXAMPLE 1

RATIONALE

The race and gender composition and occupational profiles of Organisation A's staff members reflect the same distortions as most other organisations in South Africa. White men dominate the director and senior management positions. The representation of white women improves at middle levels, but black people are still under-represented. Lower-level administrative, secretarial and housekeeping positions are the exclusive preserve of black women.

Given this profile, Organisation A believes there is a strong enough reason to adopt a set of corrective measures to encourage the greater participation of black people and women at all levels of the organisation:

Firstly, the principles and ethics of the organisation and the people who work within it demand active participation in procedures to redress past imbalances.

Secondly, affirmative action is a strategic imperative to maintain the internal and external credibility of the organisation and ensure its long-term survival.

Thirdly, the greater participation of black people and women in Organisation A is important in gearing the organisation to service clients from the full spectrum of stakeholders in society.

DESIGN PRINCIPLES

The affirmative action programme at Organisation A is framed within three guiding principles:
1. The implementation of equality of opportunity does not contradict the necessity to appoint competent people who are capable of meeting job requirements. Organisation A remains committed to maintaining high standards in the provision of its services.
2. No competent staff member will lose their job or be excluded from the possibility of promotion as a result of the equality of opportunity programme. In fact, the retention of competent current organisational members is critical to the success of a programme to diversify staff members. Their absence would not only impair the present effectiveness and impact of the organisation, but incumbent staff have a critical role to play in managing and mentoring new or newly promoted staff.
3. The implementation of equality of opportunity at a regional level should be sensitive to the fact that the balance of constituencies that Organisation A attempts to influence differs regionally. It is likely to continue to do so, reflecting the regional threats to democracy.

DEFINITION

The working definition for the affirmative action programme is as follows:

> A set of temporary policies designed to ensure equality of opportunity at
> Organisation A activated through the recruitment, selection, training and
> promotion of competent black people and women focusing particularly on
> developing such competencies amongst current staff members.

GOALS

1. To remove all discriminatory practices, implicit or explicit, in Organisation
   A resource policies and practices.
2. To ensure that within five years the composition of Organisation A
   approximates, at junior-middle management level and above, the racial and
   gender composition of South African society.

   In order to measure progress towards this goal, the following medium-term
   targets have been adopted to be achieved within two-and-a-half years. (Figures
   in brackets indicate current representation.)

   - Director and senior management positions: 60 percent black (44
     percent), 40 percent female (12 percent).
   - Junior and middle management positions: 60 percent black (44
     percent).

   Progress in meeting these targets will be assessed within two-and-a-half
   years, after which a new set of targets will be adopted for the next five-year
   period.
3. The development of internal staff members through a structured training
   and development programme.

PROGRAMME

The suggested programme to reach these goals has seven components which
may be implemented simultaneously.

1. APPOINTMENTS

- Unless no suitable candidate can be recruited, all vacant director and
  senior management positions should be filled by black people and/or
  women. They should have the potential to meet the requirements of the
  job description.
- Unless no suitable candidate can be recruited, all vacant junior and
  middle level management positions should be filled by black people.

They should have the potential to meet the requirements of the job description.

- Should the above conflict with the internal promotion policy preference, the selection committee should decide each case on its merits and may refer the matter to the chief executive.
- These provisions apply equally to contract staff.

2. RECRUITMENT

Where it is necessary to recruit people externally, the following guidelines should be followed to attract a greater proportion of black and women applicants.

- It is the immediate supervisors' role to ensure that all avenues of recruitment are actively explored.
- Advertisements for new staff must be placed in newspapers and publications that target the black population.
- In order to strengthen Organisation A's effectiveness in certain areas, advertisements may reflect culturally biased recruitment criteria such as fluency in certain languages or familiarity with, or access to, the black communities in which the organisation works.

3. SELECTION

In order to mitigate against the problem of cultural bias in selection procedures at Organisation A, and to promote a greater proportion of black and women appointments, supervisors are required to ensure that:

- Selection panels include black and white people and men and women.
- A candidate's competence must be assessed not only in terms of his/her ability or potential to perform according to a narrow job description, but also in terms of supporting strategic objectives and shifting client profiles. For example, a candidate may be assessed in terms of his/her ability to achieve desired outputs, as well as in terms of his/her ability to interact with diverse groups, and his/her understanding of and contacts with key stakeholder and experience of the dynamics of change at a grassroots level.
- Instead of the rigid specification of formal education and experience qualifications for a post, a selection committee must determine the outputs for a post. Candidates should be asked to specify why they would be able achieve these outputs. Rigid formal education criteria tend to exclude potentially competent candidates.

4. NOTICE PERIOD

Permanent staff members at director and senior management level and above are required to submit written notice of resignation to the national human resource manager two calendar months in advance. This is to ensure that the organisation has sufficient time to secure and train suitable replacement.

5. PROMOTION AND DEVELOPMENT POLICY

Identification of potential and training, in line with strategic plans and staff development, should continually take place so that a pool of potential people who can be promoted is created.

Preference for all job openings should be given to internal candidates. If no staff member currently has the skills to be appointed to a position, a staff member with sufficient potential should be identified and trained and developed to fill the position.

Urgent attention will be given to the development and promotion of secretarial and administrative staff along defined administrative and/or managerial and specialist career paths through:

- Updating job descriptions and positions based on implicit job growth.
- Creative restructuring of departments, in line with the strategic objectives of the region, to create as many opportunities for development and promotion as possible.
- Basic training in human resource management and affirmative action for the directors and senior managers.

6. OUTSIDE PURCHASES

A committed attempt will be made by all offices to source outside purchases from competitive black and women-owned firms. Some data on alternative purchasing options may be derived from the local Small Business Development Corporation, the Foundation for African Business & Consumer Services and the Get Ahead Foundation.

7. HUMAN RESOURCES POLICY TEAM

A permanent human resources policy team will be formed consisting of staff members from each of the regional/departmental offices. It will be representative of the gender, race and skills in Organisation A. The group will:

- Advise the human resource manager, the directors and senior managers on the development and implementation of the equality of opportunity plan.
- Provide policy advice on racial and gender sensitivity.
- Address issues of race and gender in an ongoing way in the organisation.

MONITORING AND EVALUATION

The affirmative action programme will be monitored and evaluated, on a regional basis, in June each year.

The monitoring exercise, to be conducted by the national human resource manager, will include:

- A survey of attitudes and perceptions of staff members towards the programme, based on interviews with a range of staff members throughout the organisation.
- A progress report on meeting the medium-term employment goal.
- A monitor showing adherence to policy changes in selection, recruitment and notice period clauses.
- Induction, support and development offered to new staff.
- Work-force succession planning, promotion and development, especially for women and black staff.
- Promotion, training and development especially for administrative and secretarial staff.
- Efforts to source outside purchases from black and women-owned firms.

ROLES AND RESPONSIBILITIES

1. THE CHIEF EXECUTIVE

The chief executive is ultimately responsible and accountable for Organisation A's affirmative action process and its milestones. The chief executive is also the highest executive authority on all issues relating to affirmative action in Organisation A.

2. THE NATIONAL HUMAN RESOURCES MANAGER

The human resources manager will monitor external recruitment and promotions and ensure that the organisation's equality of opportunity policy is rigorously pursued.

S/he will evaluate progress on equality of opportunity annually, report to the directors and board meeting and receive, review and evaluate, in confidence, complaints arising from the equality of opportunity programme. The chief executive should be informed in writing of any disputes not resolved informally. The chief executive or the national human resource manager may choose to refer a matter to the human resource policy team for resolution.

3. DIRECTORS

Directors, as line managers, are responsible for the implementation of affirmative action in their region as contained in the above paragraphs on appointments, recruitment, selection, promotions and development and outside purchases.

Progress towards meeting the programme components will form part of each regional director's evaluation conducted by the national management team.

4. HUMAN RESOURCES POLICY TEAM

As in point 7 above. (See page 173.)

EXAMPLE 2

1. DEFINITION OF AFFIRMATIVE ACTION

Affirmative action is a process designed to achieve equal employment opportunities. In order to achieve this goal, the barriers in the workplace that unfairly restrict employment and promotion opportunities have to be systematically eliminated.

2. OBJECTIVE

Organisation B recognises that because of inequalities in the apartheid education system, and race and sex discrimination in the educational and employment opportunities to women and black men, it needs to take positive steps to eliminate discrimination and to provide equal opportunities in its own work-place.

In order to enhance the representation of under-represented categories of people in the various posts within the organisation, it has put in place an affirmative action policy.

3. CONSULTATION

The company will make this policy and any subsequent changes to it available for discussion by all staff members.

Once a year a workshop will be held at which staff members' views on staff development, and affirmative action as a component of it, will be elicited and discussed.

Convenors of such workshops must make it clear that open and frank discussion and criticism are welcome and will have no negative repercussions.

There will be an affirmative action task group consisting of elected employees.

4. RESPONSIBILITY FOR THE POLICY

The company takes the view that affirmative action is a line management responsibility, ie that it forms an integral part of its core functions.

The general manager will be responsible for the implementation and success of the policy. S/he will report to the membership on progress made annually. S/he may delegate responsibility on a day-to-day basis to one of the directors, but remains ultimately accountable.

Implementation of affirmative action within their area of responsibility is one of the functions of all supervisory staff. It shall be inscribed in their job descriptions. They will be evaluated on their performance in this area in the same way as they are evaluated in connection with their other functions.

The affirmative action task group will act as an advisory body to the general manager and will be consulted by her/him on all matters pertaining to the policy. The affirmative action task group will meet once a month with the general manager.

5. EMPLOYEE PROFILE

Organisation B will carry out an audit of its employees that will be updated at suitable intervals. The audit will establish the qualifications and experience of all staff, including that which may not be directly relevant to their present position. The audit will include an accurate job description for each post.

The audit will identify staff who have potential, who could be trained or who already fulfil the criteria for promotion or sideways movement that will enhance their experience.

The profile will be classified by race and sex (for example, black women will be recorded separately from black men and not homogenised as "blacks"). This will be used to monitor progress in implementing affirmative action.

6. REVIEW OF PERSONNEL POLICIES AND PRACTICES

Organisation B will, every three years, review all existing practices, using, to inform this, a staff survey to assess perceptions and attitudes.

Organisation B will maintain a data-base to record in-house and external training, and address any sex or race bias in the provision of training opportunities.

Organisation B will ensure that unfair pay differences between men and women or between blacks and whites are not disguised either as separate grades or by confining them to lower segments of the pay scales.

7. SELECTION PROCEDURES

All vacant positions will be advertised.

External advertisements will be placed in media appropriate to the position but which will also attract applications from under-represented categories.

Job advertisements will contain the statement that "applications will be particularly welcome from black women and men".

All selection committees will have, amongst their members, at least one women and at least one black person. If Organisation B does not have such a person who is appropriate for the particular post under consideration, an appropriate person will be brought in from outside.

This committee will draw up the criteria for the job based on a thorough job description. It will take care that no unnecessarily high qualifications are demanded nor experience that is not strictly appropriate, especially where these might preclude a higher proportion of women or black people from consideration.

The shortlist of people selected for interviews will contain at least one black person and/or one women. Problems in meeting this will be reported to the general manager for resolution.

If no person from an under-represented category is selected for a post, a report of the committee's deliberations will be made to the general manager.

Care will be taken in asking questions in interviews. No questions that might discriminate unfairly against women, gays, parents or married people may be asked.

8. SETTING OBJECTIVES

Organisation B will set itself reasonable and achievable objectives according to which its success in implementing this policy will be evaluated.

The time frame for achieving these objectives will incorporate reasonable deadlines for interim objectives.

Targets will include the following:

- The number of blacks and women who will participate in training programmes each year.
- The number of people who will be moved out of non-career into career positions.
- The number of people from each under-represented category in each of the job levels in Organisation B.

In setting each target and time frame, Organisation B will indicate how it is to be assessed and who will be the individual responsible for attaining it.

9. MONITORING AND EVALUATION

Supervisors and managers will report on this area of their activity in the same way as they do on other areas of activity.

The awarding of bonuses and promotions to supervisors and managers will take into account their performance in implementing this policy.

The personnel audit will be updated annually and used as a basis for reporting on progress.

The affirmative action task group will be consulted by the general manager on monitoring and evaluating the policy, and will be given access to all the relevant information.

10. INDEPENDENT SUPPLIERS

Organisation B will make every attempt to deal with organisations and companies that recognise and support trade unions and which address the needs of the historically disadvantaged categories, especially black people (women and men), in their own policies and practices.

EXAMPLE 3

A key element in Company C's mission statement is "to create a climate in which all our human resources, in particular those disadvantaged by circumstances and lack of past opportunities, can develop their abilities to the full".

This recognises that the future success of Company C's business will be strongly dependent upon the maintenance and development of its management quality and skills. In turn this will require utilisation of all our human resources, and a reduction of the current imbalances in black representation at management level.

An affirmative action policy is therefore a business imperative. Affirmative action will seek to assist target groups and individuals redress the effects of past unfair discrimination in education and opportunity against any group, but particularly blacks. It will focus on recruitment and development of potential black management, and thus enable current disparity in the racial composition of management groups to be redressed.

In anticipation of significant far-reaching changes towards a more equitable education system in South Africa, which will "level the playing fields" in this area, it is probable that there will be a finite duration for an affirmative action programme. In this context, it will be appropriate to monitor and assess progress on a regular basis to ensure a return to an entirely merit-based practice as early as possible.

The objectives of affirmative action policy are:

- To increase both the quantity and upward mobility of black managers in the company by offering focused opportunity through recruitment, training and development, thus providing the capacity for managers to fully develop and demonstrate their management ability.
- To enhance the quality of business decision-making by enabling the values, perspectives and experiences of all South Africans to be taken into account.
- To secure the required management resources to meet the projected needs of the Company C business in the South African environment.
- By demonstrable progress in affirmative action, to encourage future governments not to legislate quotas that will bring with them an exclusive focus on headcounts. This will inevitably result in elements of tokenism, creating uncertainty about whether management status has been achieved through competence and merit.
- To help protect the viability of the free enterprise system by demonstrating that its economic benefits apply to all segments of the community.
- To retain a leadership position as a company employing enlightened and equitable human resource policies in the development of its employees.

Affirmative action strategies to achieve these objectives will focus on:

- Appointing black people to management positions provided they are capable of meeting the job requirements. This will involve some increase in risk-taking, but will not, by implication, impose a moratorium on the development of other races. It will ensure that competent black candidates are given consideration in the context of strengthening their critical mass in the business.
- Ensuring opportunities for attendance on graduate and management training courses for blacks to optimise their development and increase competencies.
- Seeking secondment opportunities for highest potential black managers in Company C outside South Africa. This will broaden perspectives, increase confidence and develop management leadership.
- Each operating unit proposing and agreeing its own short and long-term targets for the development of black management. Performance against targets will be seen and assessed as an integral part of the overall business plan achievement.
- Creating a business climate that encourages honesty, a striving for excellence in job performance, mutual respect and trust.
- Ensuring communication of affirmative action policies to all employees.

EXAMPLE 4

RATIONALE

- What does it hope to achieve?
- What is it?
- How & who?
- What are the consequences?

SOCIAL IMPERATIVE

SOUTH AFRICA'S SCHOOL ENTRIES IN 1990 (IN THOUSANDS)

Africans	1291
Whites	86
Coloureds	108
Asians	25

ECONOMIC IMPERATIVE

SOUTH AFRICA'S COMPETITIVE POSITION

1. Singapore
2. Hong Kong
3. Taiwan
4. Malaysia
5. Chile
6. Korea
7. Thailand
8. Mexico
9. Venezuela
10. Indonesia
11. South Africa
12. Hungary
13. India
14. Brazil
15. Pakistan

RANKING OUT OF 14 MIDDLE-INCOME DEVELOPING COUNTRIES:

Infrastructure	5
Finance	6
Management	7
Science & technology	7
Domestic economic strength	11
Internationalisation	13
Government	14
People	14

(Source: *World Competitiveness Report* 1993)

POLITICAL IMPERATIVE

Affirmative action legislation in new democracies

BUSINESS IMPERATIVE

Company D views affirmative action as a business imperative that must be provided for in the budget. Stakeholders want it and the market demands it. In order to maintain its efficiency and enhance its competitiveness, Company D must broaden the diversity of its work-force across all disciplines and organisational levels.

THE DESIRED END STATE

Through this process Company D will ultimately reach a stage where:
- Race, gender and creed have no effect on employment opportunities.
- The organisation values and cherishes its cultural diversity.
- Performance and ability are the only criteria by which employees and potential employees are judged.
- The organisation is viewed as having credibility and legitimacy.

This end state will be made possible by ensuring that by the year 2000 at least 50 percent of all staff in C Upper positions to F band levels on the Paterson grading system are black South Africans.

COMMITMENT

Company D has made progress in addressing the inequities of the past. We are committed to transforming the demographic profile of our business so as to more realistically reflect the community in which we conduct our business. This is a key business priority and it will be achieved through a programme of affirmative action. Key performance indicators will be set and progress in meeting them will be measured.

COMPANY D'S STANCE ON AFFIRMATIVE ACTION

Company D recognises the results of past discriminatory practices and the barriers created against blacks (including coloureds and Asians) by the system, and in line with the national changes taking place will:
- Ensure that affirmative action is seen as a means to an end.
- Introduce a strategy, policies and practices aimed at altering the racial and gender profile of Company D to be more representative of the nation as a whole.
- Support black South African small businesses and encourage companies with which it does business to do the same.
- Remove any remaining discriminatory practices regarding equality of employment.

WHITE WOMEN

White women do not fall in the same category as blacks. Company D regards blacks as the primary beneficiaries of affirmative action because of their disadvantaged background. The company is, however, addressing gender inequality by opening up opportunities for women of all races to enjoy the same benefits as men.

TOKENISM

Company D will not make token appointments. Appointing black people on the basis of potential should not be misinterpreted as tokenism, as competency will still be fundamental.

TIME SPAN

A fundamental shift in the race and gender profile of Company D will be achieved by 1996, and further progress will be made by the year 2000. A series of interim targets and milestones will be used to monitor the process.

IMPACT OF AFFIRMATIVE ACTION

This programme must provide immediate and meaningful benefits to black South Africans.

From now until December 1996, recruitment of people to Company D, including bursars and trainees, will give preference to black South Africans. More emphasis will be placed on internal development of staff.

Company D acknowledges that many blacks who had great potential were never offered an opportunity to demonstrate their leadership abilities. Blacks who meet the basic requirements for the job will therefore be appointed, with an emphasis on potential rather than on experience.

From now until December 1996, black South Africans, if judged to have the basic requirements for the job, will be given preference with regard to promotion. This does not mean that there will be no more white promotions — there will be.

Company D will actively create space for blacks in the leadership structures in the organisation.

As part of space creation initiatives, white employees may not necessarily remain in their present portfolios/jobs. Any movement of staff will be done in a fair and equitable manner and in consultation with the affected employees. In exceptional cases employees may elect to separate from Company D with benefits in order for space to be created for black South Africans. This will be done on a voluntary basis and by mutual agreement.

Company D recognises that, particularly in the next few years, the future aspirations of white males may be affected by affirmative action. Innovative ways and means will be developed to deal with this.

Attempts to disrupt the affirmative action process will not be tolerated. Company D recognises, however, that there may be some resistance to this programme. It is determined to overcome resistance through consultation and reassurance and by stressing the business imperative.

Company D recognises that the objectives of affirmative action will not be achieved overnight. It will take time, but this should not be used as an excuse to delay the process. Company D expects to see a significant change in the profile of its work-force, particularly at all levels of management and professional structures.

FACILITATION AND COMMUNICATION

A communication process reporting on progress, stimulating debate and facilitating the learning phase through which the organisation will have to go will support the affirmative action programme.

As affirmative action is a "hearts and minds" issue, it requires a change of attitude, and a commitment to make it happen. Current interventions aiming to facilitate this change process should be implemented by the organisation. The rationale for change should be constantly communicated to employees.

A FRAMEWORK FOR ACTION

To achieve the shift in pace that is demanded by this strategic priority and business imperative, the following have been put in place:
- A team of corporate advisers on affirmative action will play a leading role as facilitators, advisers and a support team. This team will have an advisory, consulting and monitoring role, using established key performance indicators. They will also be responsible for developing the appropriate learning opportunities and interventions that support the process.
- The Company D organisational groups must develop and implement their own programmes in line with Company D's objectives and desired end state. Each group has its own unique work environment that cannot be impacted by a blanket programme. The chief executive will lead this initiative and delegate responsibilities accordingly.
- As this is a corporate priority, senior managers will have the affirmative action plan included in their performance contracts, supported by time-bound, quantifiable targets against which their performance will be measured.
- The accountability for affirmative action lies with the chief executive and the management board. The executive director will be the custodian of the process.

CONCLUSION

Progress has been made throughout the organisation and positive results are already evident. This position document sets a direction aimed at accelerating the process of affirmative action and enabling managers to build on what has already been achieved.